From Marketing Expert and Huffington Post Contributor
Sarah A. O'Leary

BrandWashed
Why the Shopper Matters More Than What You're Selling

Copyright © 2011 Sarah A. O'Leary.

All rights reserved. No part of this book may be reproduced, stored, or transmitted by any means, whether auditory, graphic, mechanical, or electronic, without written permission of both the publisher and the author, except in the case of brief excerpts used in critical articles and reviews. Unauthorized reproduction of any part of this work is illegal and is punishable by law.

ISBN: 1463573359
ISBN-13: 9781463573355

Table of Contents

The Dangers of Brand Lust 1

Brandwashed: A Seven-Point Primer 7

Brand vs. Shopper Marketing: How We Got Here 13

Point of Sale vs. Point of Sofa: Owning the Sell 17

Becoming Shopper-centric 21

    How to Live in Shopper-centric Space 31

    Chances Are, You're Spending Too Much on Advertising 36

    Setting Up the Sell 39

    Be Retail-centric 43

    Research in the Competitive Retail Space 44

    Sales and Marketing vs. Marketing for Sales 45

    Developing "Shoppers First" Creative Strategies 47

    Constructing Your Shopper-centric Plan 55

"And Now a Word from Our Moral Compass…" *59*

Published Articles

Sadly, There's No MBA for Imagination 65

The Marketing Genius of Erectile Dysfunction 69

Want to Sell? Know the Retail-estate 71

Marketing in Disguise 75

Overthinking to Stinking: The Dangers of Overly Complicated
    Marketing 79

Crowdsourcing: A Legitimate Marketing Resource 83

Thanks to Spam, It's Not Junk Mail Anymore 87

Nike Ad? It Should Have Held That Tiger 91

Bad News Couldn't Have Come at a Better Time for Toyota 95

Client Death by E-mail 97

Hit the Brakes on Price Breaks 101

The Ups and Downs of Product Placement 105

Take It from Ray Kroc: There's Money to Be Made in the Air 107

The Marketing of God: When Hellfire and Damnation
    Aren't Enough 111

When to Be Social and How to Use It to Sell 115

Men Are in Marketing, Women Are at Retail 117

The Dangers of Brand Lust

Brandwashed (def): A confused state of utter and complete denial, wherein marketers believe that the brand they create and their opinions of it are more important than the wants/needs/desires of the shopper.

Shopper-centrics (def): The logical yet seemingly renegade assertion that retail products should be built from a shopper-centric perspective that begins at the actual point of sale, not from the traditional product-centric approach shaped well outside of the purchase arena.

Let's face it: the marketing industry has been *brandwashed*. We've been living too long in product idol worship, prostrate at the feet of advertising-driven brand images. We're slaves to the almighty product "personality." We've let ourselves get swept away, dreamily pondering ad nauseam the human characteristics of inanimate objects. (I wish I had a penny for every *"If Acme Orange Juice was a person, what kind of person would Acme Orange Juice be?"* type conversation I've witnessed in the past twenty-plus years.) In simple truth, we've been spending too many hours blowing smoke up our own shorts. If we used even half as much time considering the true product owners—the shoppers—as we did on our own brilliant and heady brand musings, we'd save billions in misspent dollars and countless hours of wasted effort while increasing sales and profits.

Here's the news flash: *shoppers are the most important consideration in a marketing cycle,* and they don't spend countless hours wondering if their yogurt is "perky yet confident, not afraid to share its opinion but not a gossip, sporty but not a tomboy, with a hint of mischievous independence." If we have our brand blinders on, chances are we're talking to ourselves. Shoppers are the ultimate owners of the product—they buy it, quite literally—and they make the vast majority of their purchase decisions in-store.

Rather than starting in the corporate boardrooms with our ad guys deeply considering the emotional truths of a bar of soap, we need to focus on the purchaser and her concrete wants, needs, and desires. What does she need/want/desire from her soap? Can we provide a product that delivers the right answers to her? What does her shopping environment look like? What do our competitors say to her at the most important moment—the moment of purchase impact? How can we win the support of the retailers?

Once we answer these and a host of other shopper-centric and retail-centric questions, we can develop in-store strategies and product advertising that make sense for the shopper. And, as a result of looking to advertising last rather than first, we won't spray countless dollars of marketing buckshot over various forms of media hoping something will stick. We'll be more targeted, because we'll start where sales happen—in the mind of the shopper while in the retail environment. If we start there, we'll only spend on advertising as necessary to round out an overall marketing strategy.

Whereas the notion of beginning the marketing process with the shopper might cause many brand managers to quake in their respective boots, logic is firmly on the side of a shopper-centric and retail-centric marketing approach. Regardless of how memorable your TV spot or enormous your media spend or massive your awareness numbers, your product is worthless until it is purchased.

Kellogg's® isn't the ultimate owner of its products. Wal-Mart® shareholders don't profit until shoppers purchase products and services and this hits the bottom line. Coca-Cola® employees are merely the keepers of the brand. Until a product or service is purchased at retail, it is valueless. When shoppers choose to engage or disengage a brand, they are determining its fate. Shoppers are the brand champions, and their experiences at retail are the most important element of a product's marketing life cycle.

Without a shopper-centric platform at retail, even the best-branded and advertised products risk failure. The vast majority of consumer products decisions are made in the retail environment. Approaching marketing from a shopper's point of view that begins in the purchase environment shifts the ownership from corporate to the shopper, where it belongs.

Some of McDonald's® most noteworthy, long-term successes came from understanding its shoppers, not from its deep well of brand advertising. Many doubted the strategy, even within corporate, when it launched Play Monopoly® at McDonald's in the late '80s. What did a game have to do with selling more burgers? McDonald's understood the needs/wants/desires of its shoppers, and ignored convention. Decades later, it is still on the menu at one of the most successful shopper-focused brands in history.

If Wall Street investors and shareholders realized that potentially billions of dollars are wasted on ineffective advertising plans and poor strategic choices annually, closer attention would certainly be paid to marketing and sales strategies and campaigns. Given the current economy and increased competition for every shopper dollar, smart spending is more critical to brand success than ever before.

Purchasers buy retail products in-store, not typically while watching television commercials or reading magazines or driving by billboards. Yet, marketers spend billions of dollars annually on advertising rather than in the retail environment. Significantly less is spent where purchases are made, and few if any marketing strategies begin with the shopper and her experience within the retail environment. The focus should begin where the majority of purchase decisions are made, not end there.

Without a grounded, shopper-centric understanding of the competitive retail environment, products risk silence at the register. The shoppers are the owners of products (they *buy them*, quite literally), not agencies or brand managers, and therefore must be at the forefront of marketing consideration. While all competent marketers claim to make it their business to understand the mind-set of the shopper, they are first and foremost concerned with their brands. It is far more important to understand the shopper and her/his retail experience with the brand if marketers hope to sell more.

Sales success is dependent on identifying the shoppers' engagement and reaction to products within a sea of thousands of competitive retail messages. Purchasers own the products. Retailers own the real estate. If marketing decisions are made in an ivory tower vacuum at corporate rather than from a shopper mind-set within the aisles of the store, the product risks sales failure.

Like shoppers, retailers are a critical piece of the marketing puzzle and need to be part of a product's overall marketing strategy. Retailers are realizing the power of their "retail-estate" (i.e., viewing their stores as valuable real estate to manufacturers) and the importance of delivering unique experiences to their shoppers. When a major retailer asks a manufacturer, *"What are you going to do for me in-store?"*, it is not typically focused first on product advertising. *"Why will my shopper care? How is it different from what you give my competition? Why should I give you my prized real estate? How is it in keeping with my overall shopper messaging during that calendar slot? How is it unique to my retail environment?"* These are the questions retailers ask, not how many tickets they can get for the big game or when the next image ad campaign for the product launches.

Advertising is, without question, important to the success of a myriad of products and services. However, it should be used as support for shopper-centric and retailer-centric efforts in-store. A scan of the titles of the industry's most popular trade publications shows the industry's misguided focus: *Adweek. AdAge. Mediaweek. Brandweek. Promo.* Even the *New York Times* has a *Media and Advertising* section. We still think that an advertising and product-centric focus drives products, when in truth shoppers do. The biggest voices of the industry should be called *Shopperweek* or *ShopperAge*. When we give ourselves the correct target, we will hit the bull's-eye more often.

Thanks in large part to technology, the advertising landscape has changed drastically in the past several years and big media buys aren't as effective as they once were. Cable, TiVo®, the Internet, new product competition, and the emergence of the retailer voice has changed the marketing landscape forever, making the shopper the obvious key focal point for product success. Advertising as the start of the marketing process, or even as the most important element of the marketing process, is an outdated and flawed belief.

Recently, a client was facing a loss of market share to a host of competitors. The advertising spend in support of his product was over fifty million dollars annually, much more than the competitor that was nipping at his product's heels. After meeting with his ad agency, the client decided on a solution: more advertising. As a category leader that had been around for over forty years and advertised heavily, shoppers already knew the brand's name. The client failed to realize that more advertising wasn't going to solve his sales problem. The shopper didn't need more advertising; she needed the brand to consider what she wanted from her purchase experience. Simply being made aware of the product through mass media—directed at the consumer, not the shopper—wasn't enough. Further, the client wasn't thinking about why his key retailers weren't pushing his product. Unfortunately, he increased his advertising spend, and got a minor and temporary sales lift and a dismal Return on Investment (ROI). If he had spent even one-tenth of his advertising dollars on shopper-centric strategies that appealed to the purchaser and the retailer, he would have greatly improved his sales results.

By beginning brand development in the shopper's environment, marketers will save money. If you are winning within the retail environment, an environment that doesn't require huge advertising budgets or media spends, you might actually be able to spend less on advertising and still garner better results.

As marketers, we need to find the epicenter of the shopper experience and build our brands from that point outward. If convention is brand to shopper, it needs a reversal. The brand owners have needs/wants/desires, and it's about time we recognize them.

Brandwashed:
A Seven-Point Primer

Point 1
Companies Don't Own Products, Shoppers Do

Corporations and shareholders don't own products. Shoppers own products every time they purchase. Shopper-centric thinking, rather than product-centric thinking, is crucial for successful product engagement. The most important relationship is between the shopper and the product, and the most critical time is at the exact moment of potential purchase.

Why is this important? Because if a manufacturer feels it is the owner, it risks placing more emphasis on its own internal biases rather than concentrating on the true owner, the purchaser. If you wrap yourself up in the flag of your brand, you lose the perspective necessary to deliver on the wants/needs/desires of the shopper.

Brand-centric thinking often has been a thorn in the side of the American automotive industry, which has typically been slow to react to shoppers. Lee Iacocca made his mark as an idea maverick, in large part because he did something crazy—he listened to what the shoppers wanted, first and foremost, and made Chrysler® react to it. His ideology was one of listening and creating rather than creating and pushing. By realizing who the potential product owners were, he could deliver cars that met the wants/needs/desires of car shoppers.

Point 2
The Function of Marketing Is to Sell Products and Services

Selling more products should be the focus of every member of a marketing team. While shopper awareness of your product is critical, it is worthless without sales. (I have yet to find a product that only wanted awareness.) Seeing the shift in spend from advertising to marketing, many ad agencies are attempting to reposition themselves as brand stewards. Advertising—letting people know through various media channels about your product—is only a supporting point to the greater marketing paradigm. Shopper engagement at point of sale is where all marketing strategy should begin, not end.

If marketing or advertising agencies are setting goals for awareness or traffic results and not tying success to sales, there's a good chance they feel that their approach can't deliver sales. By hedging their bets, they hope to remain relevant within the marketing paradigm and protect their own revenue streams. Although it may be impossible to predict sales results, you should always set quantifiable sales goals. The only reason to market is to sell.

When forming strategies, you'll hear a host of objectives that marketers will want to meet:

> "We have to drive traffic." Why? To sell.
> "We need to build awareness." Why? To sell.
> "We must increase distribution." Why? To sell.

If the objectives you set don't include the sell, you're risking half-baked executions resulting from incomplete sales goal setting. It is imperative to keep the focus where it belongs—on compelling shoppers to purchase products or services.

Point 3
If You Don't Win At Retail, You Fail

When you throw a pebble in a pond, the point of impact experiences the most energy. The further the waves from the point of impact, the lesser the energy. In marketing, the most critical point of engagement happens when the shopper is making the purchase decision. By putting too much time and effort into advertising and branding first, potentially miles and hours or days away from the shopper's retail experience, you risk misspent dollars and sales failure.

Research shows that approximately 70 percent of packaged goods purchase decisions are made at retail. Marketers must consider when and where the shopper is making his/her purchase decision, and spend their marketing funds accordingly. If 80 percent of products in your category are in-store decisions made by shoppers, is that where 80 percent of your marketing focus lies? If not, what percentage? If you're putting 80 percent in advertising when 80 percent of the decisions are being made at retail, you're suffering from a bad case of fuzzy math. Balance is key to successful marketing campaigns, and "fishing where the fish are" is the most basic of strategies.

It is critical to consider your shopper and the competitive retail landscape first, your retailer second, your sales force third, supportive advertising fourth, and your face on the cover of *Adweek* dead last. If you do, you'll spend less money with greater return.

Point 4
Understand the Difference Between a Shopper and a Consumer

Until fairly recently, the marketing industry used the term *consumer* as the umbrella that included both shopper and/or consumer. In the majority of grocery, drug, general merchandise, and apparel environments, the purchaser is female, probably a mom and/or wife, and she may or may not be the consumer. She's not eating the Go-GURT® or

Lucky Charms®, but she may be eating macaroni and cheese with the kids.

When Suzie Shopper is the shopper but not the consumer, she's operating in maternal or spouse mode, trying to provide the best solutions for her family. When she's the sole consumer (e.g., beauty products), she is wearing a different shopper/consumer hat. When she's buying for the family, she approaches the purchase from another mind-set. Realizing what point of view (POV) the shopper or shopper/consumer has gives marketers the understanding necessary to deliver successful, targeted marketing solutions. Depending on the product, the consumer can have very little to a critical effect on the shopper's product/service decision. If the consumer has a considerable effect on the purchase decision, his/her role must be considered in the advertising and out-of-store marketing plans. If the shopper's opinion is the determining factor, she must be the focus of the advertising strategy. In all cases, however, the person pushing the cart must be the one who is won over at the point of purchase.

Point 5
Marketing "Ownability" Is Not a Shopper Concern

Shoppers don't care if a company can claim a marketing campaign or partnership as uniquely its own. Instead, shoppers simply want a compelling reason to take a very specific action—purchase. If you are one of ten companies partnering with the NCAA for the March Madness basketball tournament, for example, the shopper won't avoid your product based on a lack of originality or repetition if the concept is solid and delivers to the shopper a real reason to engage.

A client asked, "How can we own *American Idol*?" Well, you can't. You can use the entertainment property to execute an engaging program that keys into a want/need/desire of your shopper and increase your potential for purchase, but you can't own something that is not yours. In the industry we call it borrowed equity, as we're borrowing the equity of something else in hopes of increasing sales.

The shopper doesn't care if you can "own" it, so you shouldn't. Marketers get wrapped up in whether or not the shopper dreams of being the next *American Idol* winner and thinks of peanut butter cups at the same time—not the shopper. The purpose of borrowed equity is to use something the shopper or her family loves to bring attention and sales to your product; it's not to magically transplant the same adoration shoppers have for a property to your product. People don't think the same way about Michael Jordan as they do about Wheaties®, but the two together may motivate a purchase.

Certainly, marketers need to avoid a complete disconnect between the product and a potential partnership. In some instances, a product can be temporarily adapted to be more closely tied, showing a co-ownership between product and property, giving the brand an opportunity to create new news in the retail environment. Cheetos® and its partnership with the movie *Shrek* won kids over by turning their mouths Shrek green. Knowing that kids would love the green, Frito-Lay® and retailers saw the green in their horizon and engaged the promotion. Did Frito-Lay own Shrek? No, but certainly it found a way to maximize the relationship. Shopper Mom engaged, possibly because she loved Shrek or she knew it would make her a hero with her kids. It was a home run for Cheetos, retailers, and the movie property, giving it an alternate avenue of exposure.

Point 6
If You're Starting with Advertising, You're Grabbing the Wrong End of the Fire Hose

Considering shoppers within the purchase environment first is key to the development of the most efficient and effective marketing strategies. By understanding the shopper at the point of purchase, you can better develop a branding and advertising strategy that will deliver on her wants/needs/desires. And, if you win the war at retail, you'll have to spend less on media and advertising.

When brand managers begin with the branding and ad campaign, they risk filling the airwaves and magazines with a shotgun blast of buckshot marketing. Spreading mass shot in hopes that the right shopper will be hit at the right time is too risky a venture for most products. Whereas advertising and branding is critical for the success of a variety of products (especially new product introductions), it is the most expensive form of marketing. It should be used as needed in support of the greater marketing campaign. Every dollar that isn't wasted is another dollar that may be spent on targeted marketing initiatives or given back to investors.

Point 7
If You're Selling to a _____ Shopper, Be Led By _____ Creative Marketers

In the 1970s, forward-thinking companies hired African American and Hispanic advertising agencies to reach specific minority audiences because they believed the minority agencies were uniquely qualified to reach their respective ethnic audiences. It was genius, and paid big dividends for the companies who hired agencies such as Conill and Burrell to engage consumers and shoppers.

However, when it comes to the largest purchasing population of all, women, marketing decision makers are overwhelmingly male. Corporations were quick to realize the need for targeted, like-minded voices to reach specific ethnic groups, but failed to use the same rationale to reach the largest shopper audience.

It is safe to say that men understand other men regardless of ethnicity better than men understand women. If you're going to try to reach women, have experienced female marketers lead the charge. This is not to say that men can't sell women, but rather that women understand women most intimately. If you're going after skateboarding, video- game-playing boys, look to young adult males to help you understand the mind-set.

Brand vs. Shopper Marketing: How We Got Here

When the advertising agencies first arrived on corporate earth, times were good. Shoppers weren't inundated with thousands of messages every time they went to the grocery store. There simply weren't that many competitive choices in most product categories, and simply conveying the brand information and attributes often worked. Retailers weren't demanding unique marketing plans and strategies for their shoppers. Marketers only had to get the word out that their product existed and watch the register ring.

Over the years, this paradigm has shifted significantly. Shoppers have choices, and they make most of them at retail. The industry, however, is slow to change, if not outright opposed to it. Delivering to the shopper what she wants isn't always "sexy" to the marketers or ad execs. But sales must be the overarching goal of any marketing plan.

Traditional advertising, a multibillion-dollar industry, isn't delivering shoppers in the way it once did. In the past, marketers and retailers could get by with considering their own personal opinions and interests more than those of their shoppers. Marketing departments of soup companies don't tie in with pro football players because moms are such huge fans, but because they are, and they believe the sales force and the retailers are. Yet, Mom is the one who puts the soup in the cart, making her the most important consideration.

Logic rather than the limelight must be the guiding force within a "marketing for sales" strategy. Most large retailers are governed by shareholders, and are under growing pressure to increase sales and profits. Simply giving a retailer football tickets in exchange for an in-store display is increasingly a thing of the past. More moms might be swayed with offers that deliver to their wants/needs/desires.

An increase in frequency of marketing department personnel changes has had an adverse effect on how products are sold. Gone are the days when a marketer might stay with his company for his entire professional life, being guided by both long- and short-term goals. In today's environment, many executives look to short-term "big bangs" that afford them the opportunity to job jump their way up corporate ladders. For those looking to make personal news, less glitzy and possibly more logical approaches to marketing will not deliver the right fodder for one's resume. Instead, some look to create programs that will deliver a front-page photo on *Adweek* rather than a significant sales increase. (If you do it correctly, the sales figures might not even be in by the time you leave.)

With mid-level and top corporate marketing jumps often come regime changes, which upend current marketing and advertising agencies. Unlike corporate/agency relationships of yore that may have lasted decades, agencies are in constant battles to hold on to their clients. When agencies change, invariably the messaging around the product changes as well. As an industry, we're in a place of constant uncertainty. Fighting for a relationship with a client can put the shopper message in danger. By feeling a need to create a big bang for the client, agencies can lose sight of the real need, to sell the shopper on a product or service.

Will this effort speak to my shopper? Will it build rather than damage the brand? Will it have positive short- and long-term implications? Does it have staying power? Is it a unique message for my particular product or service? Will the retailer believe in the shopper message and support the product at retail? These are some of the questions that brand marketers need to ask themselves before executing brand and advertising strategies. Without a deep shopper-centric approach, they jeopardize corporate and shareholder success.

Point of Sale vs. Point of Sofa: Owning the Sell

Since the dawn of the ad man, marketers have looked to advertising to create a brand message that leads shoppers from the newspaper, magazine, billboard, radio, and/or television set, and more recently the Internet, to the store. Even with established products that shoppers know well, companies have depended on a steady, hearty diet of advertising to drive product purchase. Shoppers, retailers, and sales numbers are telling us, however, that we're holding the wrong end of the marketing fire hose. Brand advertising should be the last—not first—step to consider in the process. Rather than begin with the brand outside of the purchase environment, we need to first consider the shopper and her experience at the point of sale, where the vast majority of purchase decisions are made.

Marketers must look to first win the war where the battles take place, with the shopper at the point of purchase, not miles away armed with only a television commercial sent into the viewer's home. In all but the exception of marketing scenarios (e.g., new product introductions), it makes little logical sense to first focus most of the money and effort on the delivery of a message into an environment where purchase of a product cannot be made.

Let's say you're selling cornflakes. You're one of five companies that make cornflakes, and you've been selling the same cornflakes for years. Everyone knows that you make cornflakes. Is it most effective to attempt to reach the shopper through a TV commercial during the breakfast hour in hopes that she's watching, or when she's in the cereal aisle trying to decide which box of cornflakes to buy? Is it better to run a brand-driven print ad in a magazine that may or may not reach your shopper, or should you invest in an in-store effort that excites your retailer and gets you more shelf space? The purpose of marketing is and always will be to sell, and thus the point of sale—the retail environment—should be the launch pad for marketing strategy. And, though advertising is a critical component in the marketing of many products, it isn't where brand thinking should begin.

In a typical marketing process, a corporate brand manager first meets with his ad agency to discuss the product he wants to market. If it's a new product, the ad agency might spend months developing the product's personality and attributes. The agency or company may execute shopper research to clarify the target audience (i.e., the group that will buy the most amount of the product) and support its assumptions made about the audience. The agency will decide how to convey the product's personality and attributes via advertising, and will develop an advertising media plan to reach the shoppers it believes will be most likely to purchase the product. At some point, the advertising creative ideas may be put before a research group of shoppers to decide if the brand message works. Eventually, after the product positioning is cemented, the brand manager may work with his marketing agency to figure out how to sell the product at retail. The retailer may or may not be involved in the development or be made aware of the in-store strategy.

Without a deep understanding of the shopper within the retail environment, products risk silence at the register. The shopper is the owner of the product (she/he *buys it*, quite literally), not agencies or brand managers, and must be at the forefront of marketing consideration. Whereas all competent agencies hopefully attempt on some level to understand the mind-set of the shopper, understanding that shopper within the constructs of the retail environment is critical.

The shopper's engagement with a brand is not simply about the reinforcement of the brand positioning through constant advertising messaging. Susie Shopper isn't carrying an advertising message in her head that relates to every product she'll put in her cart. Instead, her experience and action at the point of purchase are the primary drivers of a product's success. How do we create a valuable product experience in-store that will make that shopper engage and take immediate action at the point of contact? By determining what the shopper wants and how the product can provide it, we can build a compelling message that's literally within the shopper's grasp. From there, we determine the best way to involve the retailer—an increasingly powerful part of the equation—and the sales force. After we consider shopper and retailer wants/needs/desires and analyze the competitive in-store landscape, we can create a brand strategy and advertising message that meets those needs.

For countless retail products, the purchase journey begins three feet in front of the product, not six miles away on the couch. Advertising is, and will remain, important to the success of a myriad of products. It serves as a key component in building product image and awareness, as well as an important factor in communicating promotional messaging. Without product awareness, either via media or at retail, the product is a tree that falls in the forest without a shopper in earshot. Advertising is, however, the best place to end rather than begin when developing a product's marketing strategy.

Quantifiable measurement is critical in gauging campaign effectiveness or ROI. Advertisers have long emphasized potential consumer awareness levels of the advertising as a benchmark for success. Conversely, marketing agencies running in-store campaigns are typically judged by sales increases. Now more than ever, retailers are putting more value on the power of in-store "retail-estate." If you ask any of the major retailers, the ones that actually sell the products, they will tell you their floor space and what products do with it are more valuable than a product's advertising spends.

Point of Sale vs. Point of Sofa: Owning the Sell

Consider this: an estimated one hundred million plus people walk through the doors of Wal-Mart *every week*, and are exposed to thousands of messages. Put this number against the ninety to one hundred million viewers who watched a Super Bowl and its handful of commercial messages, and there's really no comparison. Shoppers are receiving more messages from their in-store experience than from traditional media. Further, Mom isn't watching the Super Bowl ads while she's pushing her shopping cart. If a product's message doesn't come through loud and clear at the point of contact in the sea of other products and their messaging, no amount of media will save it. And, if the retailer doesn't believe the product's marketing strategy is best for his or her shoppers, it won't have the retail-estate or support necessary to increase sales. The battle to be waged is over floor tiles and shelf space, not simply awareness garnered from advertising.

Beginning the brand marketing process at retail in the shoes of the shopper instead of ending there is a renegade yet logical ideology. And, whether advertising and marketing execs agree with it or not, there is one indisputable, overarching truth of marketing:

A product is worth nothing until it is purchased.

Becoming Shopper-centric

As an executive at one of the world's largest general merchandise retailers put it, "The one driving our bus is pushing our cart." In the case of his company, almost every department was shopped primarily by women. In true shopper-centric fashion, he realized that they should be the primary focus when plotting marketing strategies. When dealing specifically with the electronics and automotive departments, however, the focus shifted to male shoppers. Standing in your shopper's shoes will guide you to successful plan mapping.

The Psychology of the Sell

Sales are the successful results of decisions made by shoppers. If you want to sell more of something, live intimately within the mind-set of your key core shoppers.

Certain products may have more than one target audience. Analyze all targets and determine the percentage of purchasing power of each audience. If your secondary audience numbers are significant, marketing dollars should be spent against the audience and the retail channel in which its members engage your product. Note that this is only if your primary marketing strategies aren't effective in reaching the secondary audience, and if the secondary audience is big enough to merit the spend. Make certain that the amount of your spend is relative to the percentage of sales the audience delivers to your product.

First and foremost, become a student of your audience and how those in it engage your brand. My agency, Logic Marketing, uses a psychologist to offer professional insights and review creative strategies to ensure we hit the sweet spot with the shopper. Utilizing all available expertise so that you deliver on shopper wants/needs/desires is another way you can nail the psychology of the sell.

Before you begin any marketing process, you have to know the shopper and see your product through her eyes. When looking to understand your shopper, there are several questions you should consider.

Who are they?

Although it has yet to be given the massive weight it deserves, the most important factor to consider is the gender of the shopper. The industry has gone to great lengths to break out the actual consumers by age, nationality/ethnicity, household income (HHI), marital status, geographics, etc. In fact, whether they are male or female is the most important part of the equation, because women and men are different emotional beings. Consider this at the top of your list, and then work through all the other pertinent demographic elements.

Before you learn every intimate detail of your brand personality, you must know who your shoppers are. Then you'll be fully prepared to mold your marketing messages to reach those consumers most efficiently and effectively.

How do they spend their days?

When not in purchase mode, where are your shoppers? Home Depot® executed a brilliant promotional campaign to reach men by understanding who and where they were. As a group, men redeem significantly fewer coupons than women. And, as a group, millions of men follow Major League Baseball. At various games, Home Depot distributed Mystery Value Gift Cards to baseball fans. Each had a value of at least one dollar, but could be worth up to one thousand dollars. In truth, this was a very cleverly disguised coupon, as the vast majority of cards were simply one dollar off a purchase.

Redemption of these gift cards came in well above what would have been witnessed with a simple coupon. In this case, Home Depot understood where men were (at the ballpark), what they would/wouldn't do, and what would be enough of a carrot to get them into its retail environment. By making it necessary for the gift cards to be scanned at checkout, and knowing that shoppers typically don't enter the checkout without a product to purchase, Home Depot almost guaranteed a sale with every mystery card scanned.

How do their actions change by season? Day part? Week part?

A mom shopping during back to school will have different purchase needs/wants/desires than the same mom will have during the winter holidays. She's the same shopper, but her priorities change throughout the year. Knowing shopping patterns will help you implement your marketing strategies at the best time for the best results.

It is also imperative to know what your key retailers will be emphasizing throughout their calendar year. By understanding their motivations, you will better equip yourself to have your product included in their marketing efforts.

There is no reason you can't try to get shoppers to purchase your products during a time they typically don't buy it, provided you accomplish your marketing goals during your key purchase cycles. A common mistake is believing that your product will sell itself during your high-impact periods, even if you don't do much marketing. This, however, is rarely the case. You must win the key periods first, and look to expand second. True, you might not need to spend as much during the times when you know you have strong sales, but you still must support your products. Shoppers have a choice in almost every category, and you have to be certain to win them at every opportunity.

Suggesting alternate product uses can be a great way to grow your purchase frequency and increase sales. Nothing helped graham crackers sales more than the invention of s'mores. In the case of Arm

& Hammer® baking soda, its value to shoppers as a deodorizer and cleaner overshadowed its use as a baking ingredient, changing the breadth of its sales opportunity.

Delivering compelling messaging to shoppers to change their habits also can be beneficial to sales. TCBY® frozen yogurt did just that when it ran a dead of winter promotion to increase sales at some of its retail stores. For every degree below freezing the temperature dropped, the stores discounted the price of frozen yogurt. By creating new news in its environment that was of interest to its shopper base, TCBY succeeded in sales generation.

What's important to them?

For many Americans, starting a savings plan was important but seemingly out of reach. Bank of America® realized this, and saw it as a means to increase the number and value of its checking and savings accounts.

In its program, Keep the Change®, shoppers who used a Bank of America check card automatically deposited money in their savings account. Every time a consumer used his/her check card, Bank of America rounded up the purchase to the next dollar and transferred the difference from the shopper's checking to his/her savings account. As an added incentive, Bank of America matched the savings for the first three months and 5 percent a year after that time, with a maximum of $250 in matching funds.

Through Keep the Change, Bank of America provided shoppers a service with incentive that met their needs/wants/desires, while meeting its own corporate goals. The result was a win for both corporation and shopper.

What do they do for work? For play?

If you can find out how your shopper spends his/her time, maybe you can figure out a method to work your way in.

A Hispanic advertising agency approached a marketing agency to create experiential concepts for its automotive client. The ideas needed to center around a major pickup truck line and its professional truck racing series partnership. Two things became apparent from the research: 1) Family was important to young adult Hispanic men and very much a part of the social considerations, and 2) Hispanic men liked the idea of "tricking out" or personalizing their trucks.

The winning concept featured a family-focused affair at professional truck tour events, complete with music, rides, and tricked-out trucks. With a test-drive, visitors eighteen and older would receive a certificate for a free basic trick-out tool set from a major general merchandise retail partner. With a new car purchase, drivers would receive a complete tool set and a gift card to the retailer. In addition, retailers would display the pickup trucks in their parking lots (or inside stores), and host professional driver visits and trick-out clinics. A "Drive the Dream" sweepstakes overlay gave shoppers a chance to drive on the track where their favorite drivers raced, and to win one of five tricked-out trucks.

The advertising agency, considered the agency of record for the car company, didn't present the concept even though it did extremely well in research focus group testing. The campaign would have been given to an events or promotion agency, with the money coming out of the ad budget, which didn't sit well with them. Regardless, knowing how your shoppers live outside of the purchase environment can give you valuable clues and opportunities to draw them to purchase.

How do shoppers experience your product? What noncompetitive products do they use with your product?

By understanding what products they use beyond your product, you might find a potential partner for a cooperative marketing effort. If your shopper buys milk every week and you sell cookies, a joint effort with a milk company will deliver more opportunity to you.

Appropriate partnerships give you the opportunity for alternate means of exposure and increased sales.

When Barnes & Noble® began installing comfortable chairs and tables for shoppers in its bookstores, some experts cautioned that the corporation was turning its stores into libraries. Instead, Barnes & Noble thrived and sales increased because it brought a new and welcome level of experience to its shoppers. Understanding the wants/needs/desires of its shoppers, the corporation also pursued an innovative partnership opportunity with a major coffee retailer. Starbucks® and Barnes & Noble delivered to shoppers when they installed cafes in the bookstore retail environment. Barnes & Noble sold more, not fewer, books from the comfort of in-store furniture. Further, it successfully developed an additional revenue stream in another controversial first, serving food and beverages in a major bookstore chain. By understanding its shoppers and taking two large measured risks, Barnes & Noble drove its sales and shopper satisfaction to a new level.

What products do they buy in place of yours?

It is critical to consider why a shopper is passing on your product and choosing your competition. In some cases, there might not be a lot you can do about it (e.g., they prefer the taste of another product over yours). In many cases, it might simply be that the competition is delivering on wants/needs/desires in a way you're missing. Are they running a promotion that the shopper finds engaging? Does the shopper get an added-value bonus for purchasing their product? What is the tipping point in terms of the decision? It is imperative to realize that in most retail environments shoppers are receiving thousands of competitive messages. If your competition is delivering a message that is outperforming yours, you need to rethink your strategies.

Too often, companies look to defend and protect their products and brands at the expense of sales. "Ownability" is a term often used, referring to ownership of a brand message as the most important element to success. However, the USP (Unique Selling Proposition) or shopper offering within a competitive environment is much more important to consider. If the competition is delivering a more compelling marketing message that is leading to more sales, that message must be exceeded.

When designer jeans invaded the apparel market, top-selling Levi's® hung back and stayed with its brand message, turning a blind eye to the competition until it was nearly too late to react. Certainly Levi's wasn't a designer brand, but could have taken a myriad of steps, from purchasing a designer jeans company to hiring a designer to represent its product line to stop some of the erosion. Staying simply Levi's in the face of competition was definitely ownable, but certainly not profitable.

What causes do they support?

Knowing what pulls at the heartstrings of your shopper can give you marketing opportunities that deliver positive PR for you, great spin for retailers, and increased sales.

Products supporting causes motivate women purchasers in particular. Wilson took an existing tennis racket, turned it into a pink ribbon tennis racket in support of breast cancer research, and saw double-digit sales increases. Yoplait® yogurt's Susan G. Komen lid collection program was a sales home run, and has become an evergreen promotional effort for the company. At first, marketers could not believe it. Who on earth would want their brand associated with breast cancer? What Yoplait knew was that the shopper cared deeply about finding a cure for breast cancer. The company understood women and their attraction to helping each other. Yoplait became the yogurt that understood the shopper, and cared about women.

With a downturn in the economy, even those who would want to give to a charity will be less able to do so. If, by purchasing a product in a category they shop a donation is made to a charity they have a heart for, shoppers will feel even better about their purchase decisions.

What three issues are most important to them?

During political election cycles, the airwaves are inundated with reports of voter polls. What's most important to the majority of voters? The economy? Education? Health insurance? Politicians look to reams of data when sculpting the messages they feel will deliver on the wants/needs/desires of their audience, potential voters. The message often changes based on the audience they are addressing, so that they can cast the widest net.

If you're an automotive company and your shopper is most interested in the economy and environment, you may look to put special emphasis behind a line of fuel-efficient hybrids. Toyota® did just that with the launch of Prius®, and made record-breaking sales gains.

In a tight economy, getting more for less will outweigh quality messaging for a host of products. Starbucks felt this firsthand when economic concerns led to a severe drop-off in sales. In reaction, Starbucks launched a low-priced coffee offering in hopes of fighting off the inevitable erosion of its base.

Once the darling of food service retail, Krispy Kreme Donuts® didn't successfully anticipate or react to an anti-carbohydrate sentiment of epidemic proportions among shoppers. Because of a limited menu of offerings, the corporation wasn't able to immediately deliver a non-carb-based product line that was compelling enough to the shopper to fight off loss. Righting the ship to a place where shoppers would see it as more than a carb-laden donut shop was a difficult fight to undertake.

In contrast, Dunkin' Donuts® discovered long ago that shoppers' primary reason for visiting the chain is its coffee, not its donuts. Keeping an eye on its driver, great coffee, Dunkin' Donuts could explore other food product opportunities with its shoppers.

How often do they purchase your product, and why?

Purchase frequency is a key consideration when developing your marketing plan. If your product is purchased twice a year, a frequency-based loyalty program would not be a good idea. You might find that your hard-core shoppers are already at their purchase limit for your product. In this case, it might be wise to attempt to cast the net wider and reach shoppers who can be persuaded to increase their purchase frequency.

Before frequent flyer programs, airline passengers made decisions generally based on price, routes flown, and flight times. With the advent of the frequent flyer rewards program, travelers were given compelling reasons to become loyal to specific airlines. The more often they flew, the more perks such as free trips and cabin class upgrades they would receive from the airline. Business travelers received rewards for performing a job function, making travel a bit more tolerable.

Now, shoppers can secure airline points on everything from the car they rent to the credit card they use. And they can redeem points for hotel rooms, rentals, and a host of other perks. Understanding the shopper whys gave airlines a unique selling opportunity for their shoppers. The challenge with frequent flyer points programs is differentiation. What does one program deliver that is more compelling than the next? What does the shopper want the experience to deliver? Major airlines are getting schooled by the likes of Virgin America® and Southwest® because of what they deliver—humor, friendliness, a positive consumer experience, and loyalty programs that are unfettered. Losing sight of the shopper gives your competition opportunity.

How flexible is your marketing messaging?

The same widget can be sold to a host of audiences in a way that appeals to them, provided the marketing message can be tailored to target each specific audience. The same product sold to moms in grocery stores requires a different voice to young males in convenience stores. It might need a separate added-value promotional offering, or even a different product size offering. The more effectively you can tailor your messaging and offering to meet the wants/needs/desires of specific target audiences in specific retail environments, the better your chances to sell. Building messaging flexibility into your marketing plans should always be part of your strategic considerations.

Unfortunately, brandwashing has led a host of marketers to believe that their brand message is powerful enough to reach all potential purchasers. Would you speak the same way to a child that you do to your spouse? Do men have the same conversations with other guys that they do with women? When women are together, do they have the same discussions as they do with their children or spouse? Do shoppers in downtown Los Angeles have the same point of view about their world as shoppers in Nebraska? The more messaging can be tailored to reach key audiences, the better the product performance.

Is there a nontraditional way you can reach your shoppers to sell them?

Sometimes the sales answer lies in fishing where the fish are, which might not be where you traditionally reside.

A smaller foreign car company found through its research that college students tend to purchase from dealerships in close proximity to campus. The car company didn't have many dealerships in comparison to its competition, so it wrote off any hope of selling to the college market. Had the company created a mobile program, bringing automobiles to areas close to campuses where co-eds could have easily test-driven the vehicles and purchased them at that time, the company would have been able to increase its collegiate sales.

Some companies execute mobile tours to increase awareness. Depending on your product, however, these could be wasted dollars. Supporting your product at the point of sale is closer to the sell and therefore in most cases more valuable. With some image-based products driven by target audiences concerned with image (e.g., the Mountain Dew® Tour aimed primarily at teenage boys), sponsorships and mobile experiences may work well. One must consider, however, where the vast majority of purchases are made. If the answer is in the grocery store, aligning with snowboards on the slopes might not be the best marketing spend. A sweepstakes featuring snowboard-related prizing with special snowboard celebrity packaging that makes Mom a hero with her son at home might serve sales better.

What does your gut tell you?

Asking questions to better understand your shopper is imperative, but there is a danger in too much research at the expense of action. You need to remain fluid and flexible enough to implement programs efficiently and effectively. It is also critical to realize the limitations of research. Give it power, but use common sense as well. Research is never totally complete or infallible. Regardless of how well researched and prepared, great marketing often means taking chances.

Like anything created by the human mind, research is biased and imperfect. Too often, we as marketers can get lost in the research, and end up losing our ability to execute big ideas in the process. A CMO of a major fast-food corporation listened intently as reams of research were being presented to him. He overruled the researchers and marketers, all of whom were directing him to a safer marketing approach. It was certainly a gutsy call, and six months later he was proven right.

How to Live in Shopper-centric Space

If you really want to see how shopper-centric you are, host your next marketing concept presentation in the aisle of your top retailer, right in front of your product. In that arena, see if the ideas you are considering would form the engagement necessary to deliver on the needs/wants/desires of your shopper.

Living in shopper-centric space is a complete and total immersion. It's not simply that the shopper comes first. Instead, it's that you know the shopper and deliver on that shopper's desires within his/her retail experience in a way that's relevant to him/her.

Most major retailers know how shoppers move within their stores and what staple items they buy with regularity. They use this knowledge for product placement in the store. Have you ever wondered why milk is always in the back of the grocery store? Its placement makes shoppers walk down an aisle filled with non-staple items that might end up in their cart. Understanding shopper behavior within the purchase environment, strategic placement of items that typically end up in the cart, and breakthrough product messaging all lead to increased sales.

Although it may be tempting to live in a corporate campus contemplating the brand image in a vacuum, it is dangerous, given all that the shopper and the retailer are considering. You have to be on the field to win the game.

The Shopper Rights

Shopper experience, product attributes, and perceived value (price plus quality plus offerings) determine shopper engagement. If the equation is right for them, it will also be right for you.

Right Product

If you don't have the right product based on shoppers' wants/needs/desires, you won't be successful regardless of the marketing effort. You can't sell a napkin parachute no matter how compelling your pitch.

When Frito-Lay launched snacks made with the Proctor & Gamble® fat substitute Olestra®, it believed it had the right product, and so did the shoppers—until they experienced its harsh side effects. Thousands had diarrhea, flatulence, greasy stools, and a host of other related maladies. A snack product with a fat substitute was the right idea, but Frito-Lay most certainly had the wrong product. (A friend at the company said the product line named "WOW!" was known internally as "WHOA!") It was a multimillion-dollar disaster.

There are rare instances, too, when your added-value shopper offering can overtake your product. At the height of the Beanie Babies® craze, McDonald's ran its first of many Teenie Beanie Babies Happy Meal® promotions. Shoppers were so excited to get multiple Teenie Beanie Babies that many ordered Happy Meals with no food. McDonald's promotion was a maelstrom of activity, and proved wildly successful.

Right Time

Is your product ahead of its time? Behind the times? The sweet spot of shopper relevance is critical to success. Sometimes shoppers aren't ready for certain products, and some products run their course (we no longer have eight-track players in our cars, for example).

Living within shoppers' purchase reality requires sweet spot timing. Before you create, make certain there is a strong potential shopper base that would be willing to engage your product.

In Hollywood, timing is everything. The movie studios have a host of formulas that guide the release process. There are key times to release movies by genre, and specific "street date" (DVD release) sweet spots. As the commercial property is all they have to sell, it is crucial to get the most engagement during the best window of opportunity. And, as most movie studios rely on sponsors to add to marketing funding and cross-sell their pictures, the studios also must consider what the right timing for potential partners and key retailers will be. Releasing a movie or streeting a DVD at the wrong time can cost millions in lost sales, and can damage a studio's reputation. Knowing the best time to launch a marketing initiative, regardless of the industry, is crucial to sales.

Right Retail Environment

The retailer must believe that your product will sell within his/her retail environment during the times you've suggested. Big bags of single-serve candy sell well around Halloween, and the retailer buys accordingly. Look to make sure your retailer is on the same page as you are, and that you've taken the steps necessary to convince him/her that you are the best choice for any special programs he/she might be running within his/her environment.

Sometimes the product offered within a retail environment doesn't match the retailer's shoppers. If you go into a heavily Hispanic area and visit a grocery store, most likely you won't find pierogies in the frozen foods section. It is important to set distribution so that the right products/services are in the right environment to maximize sales efforts. In some cases a product can be adapted for differing shopper audiences, which could signal a new growth area for it. (Bilingual point-of-sale communication and packaging have proven extremely beneficial in this regard.)

The shopper must believe that the product is relevant in the environment in which it is presented to them. Shoppers don't visit the hardware store to buy milk. The audience has to want to hear your message and believe it in the place of purchase.

Right Value Proposition and Message

What value can you offer to your shopper? You can win on price, quality, or an added-value offering, such as a gift with purchase or a chance to win a million dollars. The shopper needs to believe that she is getting something more than she would from another product.

Ozarka® caught the bottled water industry by surprise when it launched a new bottle that was a different shape and made with 30 percent less plastic than its previous bottle. Ozarka's sales increased, as shoppers who were interested in the eco-friendly approach chose it. Further, by using less plastic, Ozarka lowered its production costs.

Major League Baseball parks use giveaways and special promotional event experiences as tactics to get more people to the ballparks and/or get fans there earlier. "The first ten thousand receive a free baseball courtesy of Acme Hot Dogs" means ten thousand people will go to the game early, patronizing the concessions and gift shops before the game even starts. The ball club will have the promotion paid for by the sponsor, making it a winning proposition without cost to management. At ballparks that don't sell out every game, the added value can sway fans to take in a game rather than simply watch it on TV. The ballpark's promotional calendar gives the club the opportunity to create new news, delivering successful value propositions to the fans throughout the season. Plus-ing up the shopper experience with the right value proposition can deliver new shoppers and increase the frequency with which existing shoppers purchase.

The right message comes from the heart of the shopper. It is imperative to find the cross section between the shopper's wants/needs/desires and the product's assets, and to do it more effectively than the competition.

Within the retail environment, manufacturers don't typically have a great deal of communication time with shoppers. At grocery, for example, you don't have thirty seconds of pristine advertising time to reach shoppers. Instead, experts believe you may have as little as three seconds in front of your potential buyer. It is crucial to focus messages and batten down the kitchen sink. As a rule, no more than three messages should be carried on display, and no more than two major messages on packages.

Breakthrough messaging is critical to sales success. Products need to create news within the purchase environment by calling out their assets and any new news the manufacturer can share with the potential buying audience.

The Good Housekeeping® Seal of Approval is the quintessential example of using a specific message to convey a product's trustworthiness. For shoppers looking to feel that a new product they've yet to experience is less of a gamble, the seal offers peace of mind.

The messaging on point-of-sale materials should be determined by cross-referencing the wants/needs/desires of your shoppers and product/service offerings. Further, you'll need to make sure that, if in a competitive environment, your message is stronger than that of your competition.

"Twenty percent more, FREE!" was an example of a strong value proposition/price message before falling victim to overuse. "Expert recommended" delivers on product quality, as was evidenced by the Trident® gum "nine out of ten dentists recommend" messaging of the 1970s. "FREE INSIDE!" delivers to those looking for a non-product added value. From sugared cereals to boxes of detergent to cars that come with matching luggage, this message has proven to be successful. The key is to deliver the right amount of shopper-centric messaging necessary to meet sales goals. It could be that simply showing a professional endorsement is enough. See-through packaging that reinforces quality, such as that of the category-shifting Simply Orange®, could be the answer. A one-in-four chance to win a big prize could spike sales. In a marketing calendar year, it might be a combination of messages that deliver new news to the purchase environment and increase sales. Finding the least amount of advertising messaging and promotional offerings is key to sales success.

Chances Are, You're Spending Too Much on Advertising

Traditional brand advertising isn't creating a wake. In most cases it should be having one.

Let's look at a consumer product like it's the Big Man on Campus. He's the good-looking athlete that everyone is drawn to, and there's no question that his image sells itself. The other hot commodity is the new kid in school, as he's an unexplored novelty. Now, think of how many guys like these two are in the population of man. Probably less than 1 percent. The same goes for brands that sell themselves strictly on image or novelty. For the 1 percent, brand advertising might very well be the best place to spend the majority of marketing dollars. For the other 99 percent, we need to work a little smarter.

Thanks in part to shareholders and investors and a shrinking economy, smart marketing spends are more important than ever. And, as advertising and media traditionally are the priciest elements of any marketing equation, marketers need to make certain that their spends are well managed. If the first part of a marketing spend is on advertising, chances are the shopper and her engagement within the retail landscape is getting shortchanged. Awareness without sales is worthless. Sales without media-driven awareness is possible with a strong in-store marketing strategy.

Take this example: a client was losing market share (the percentage of shoppers who chose his product over his competitor's product). His product had been a Big Man on Campus, but it had long since graduated and was seen more as a nice guy who lived down the street, without the flash he once had or would have again. The brand manager upped his advertising spend, relying on image, and still lost sales. He lacked the shopper-centric and retail-centric strategy necessary to reverse his dipping sales. The tools he had used successfully in the past were not going to benefit him in the future.

The most efficient marketing spends begin with considering the shopper at the point of purchase first. Media spends are becoming less effective in reaching target audiences, and will only wane as technology continues to improve. The retail environment, however, will remain the place to reach shoppers efficiently and effectively. Rather than the marquee player, advertising is best served as support to a shopper-centric marketing strategy.

Technology (cable, Internet, etc.), an influx of consumer products, and an ever-increasing fight for shopper mind share have lessened the role of traditional advertising within the marketing paradigm. Consumer-generated content in the under thirty-five audience is white-hot, as was witnessed by the top-performing TV spots that ran during last year's Super Bowl (the Doritos® "Crash the Super Bowl" spot being one example). TiVo and other technologies are making the watching of TV advertising optional.

What the industry has termed as "nontraditional" media (e.g., the Internet, social media) marketing is becoming the norm, as consumers are not experiencing advertising in the same way they did even five years ago.

With a depressed economy, manufacturers and retailers must fight even harder to make sales. A cooperative, targeted effort focused at retail rather than large ad spends can deliver more sales more efficiently and more effectively. Just as in physics, the most power is generated at the moment of impact.

As crazy as it may seem, most goods and services do not advertise either regularly or at all outside of the retail environment. Those companies must sell well at retail, or they risk not reaching their full potential. In-store marketing (advertising and promotions) drive shopper and retailer interest, and when successful can turn an average brand into a great one.

Understanding a shopper's purchase cycle for a product is critical, and often overlooked by brand marketers. Chances are, Suzie Shopper isn't going to buy a case of champagne unless it's around the holidays. And because the retailer knows this, he/she isn't going to want to give the product an end aisle in July or front-page placement in the store's circular. Advertising when you have the best chance of selling a product will help make the media spend more effective. Certainly, we can all try to figure out a way to sell champagne in the summer, but we might be better served to fish where the fish are in order to best manage our sales efforts.

Setting Up the Sell

Marketing Existentialism (def): A product only exists if a shopper perceives it to exist in his/her purchase reality.

Don't Hide Behind the Brand

Countless marketers who build brands away from retail make excuses to deliver on what they find engaging rather than what the shopper needs/wants/desires.

Case in point: Gatorade® inked a reported hundred-million-dollar five-year deal with Tiger Woods and launched three flavors of Gatorade Tiger. Mom, pushing her cart through retail in Iowa looking for a sports drink for her kids, wasn't going to buy one more bottle of Gatorade because of Tiger Woods. She was more motivated by what her kids wanted and what was good for them than the superstar pro golfer on the Gatorade advertising roster.

It's possible that the campaign was hoping to increase sales by delivering on the "nag factor"—kids pleading with Mom to purchase the product. Unfortunately for Gatorade Tiger, kids are most often drawn to sports heroes who represent sports they play or regularly watch. Gatorade's highly effective "If I Could Be Like Mike" advertising campaign was an example of understanding the person young kids wanted to be like—the NBA superstar of the sport they loved. By drinking his drink (and wearing his shoes), they got to be a little more like him. Kids don't play or watch golf in large numbers, making Tiger not a motivating choice for them. While Tiger is a sports superstar, he's not the right hero to reach the nag factor audience.

Another key element of the Gatorade Tiger disconnect was an actual product formula change. Gatorade Tiger has 25 percent more electrolytes than regular Gatorade. Do we believe that pro golfers like Tiger Woods need 25 percent more electrolytes than, say, the pro basketball, soccer, or football players who endorse regular Gatorade?

Would more electrolytes take a couple of swings off my golf game? In this instance, the product attributes didn't match the marketing effort.

Often, brand managers will realize that a marketing campaign is off strategy for Mom and pass it off as a retailer-focused play. "The retailer loves Tiger, so he'll give me more display." Whereas that used to be true in many instances in the past, it is certainly not the truth (or should not be the truth!) of retail today. Retailers have stockholders to report to, and can't risk their space for personal interest or gain.

Misguided strategies can also be passed off as "brand true" or ownable to the brand (e.g., Gatorade is *the* brand that the world's best athletes use). This, too, is a way to put too much of the marketer's point of view into the process. The average mom doesn't care that Gatorade has pro athletes on its roster. She wants to keep her kids happy, and make the right choices for her family. If her kids have a sports beverage preference and she sees no difference between sports drinks, the child's opinion may sway her decision-making process. A compelling retail message that delivers a distinct point of difference (e.g., Gatorade hydrates better and keeps kids safer) or motivating added value (free Gatorade sideline sports towel with purchase) that makes her a hero to her kids would deliver on Mom's wants/needs/desires and sell more product.

Make a Scene

Major manufacturers go to great lengths to create packaging and product-driven, aesthetically pleasing point-of-sale displays. Go to any division of PepsiCo® and you'll see smart-looking product displays for its various products in its offices. Go to Wal-Mart corporate, however, and you can see an entire physical in-store environmental scene set. By studying the complete competitive environment, marketers can better understand the shopper's point-of-purchase experience.

This section establishes the need for product marketers to see past themselves and consider the competitive environments in which products live in their various retail spaces. Focusing simply on how a marketer's product looks is myopic, and gives potential advantage to the competition. Most importantly, it doesn't afford manufacturers the opportunity to consider a shopper-centric point of view or see the challenges faced by the retailer. Creating a point of scene at corporate that includes the physical layout, complete with competitive product that is changed by retailer initiatives, will help product managers understand the challenges and opportunities within the marketplace.

The Importance of Legitimate "New News" in the Retail Environment

Differentiate

Special attention should always be paid to product innovation, packaging, and point-of-sale materials. Many companies introduce limited edition changes to their products—from cars to candy bars—to create shopper buzz. Within the retail space, differentiation is key. Simply Orange blasted onto the orange juice scene with a drastically different package—a clear bottle—which was noticeably different from its white carton competition. The shoppers embraced the packaging, believing it to be fresher and more wholesome based on its clear bottle.

Listen to the Shopper, and Be Ready for Change

Trending isn't always the rocket science that researchers make it out to be. More challenging, typically, is being able to change course in time to be in step with emerging shopper wants/needs/desires. Sustainability is a current trend in packaged goods marketing, thanks in large part to Wal-Mart's corporate initiative. Manufacturers who can make green statements will have more news to share with Wal-Mart, and therefore more opportunity. Wal-Mart, keying into a shopper want/need/desire, believes it can sell more products through this commitment while doing something good for the environment. Provided it can deliver the green products at the same or nominally different pricing as non-green competitors, the formula will work.

When planning a yearlong marketing calendar for a product or service, keep in mind the need for flexibility based on the shopper's changing point of view.

Deliver

If you say you're going to do something, you must do it. If you say your product is something, make sure it is. Products must deliver on their brand promises.

- Deliver on the wants/needs/desires of the shopper.
- Deliver on product/promotion offer promises.

If Standing on the Banana Peel, Spend Wisely

When sales slip, product marketers may look to an increased advertising spend to project more brand messaging to the masses. The answer lives within the confines of the retail space, with a few exceptions (competitive push, changes in branding, etc.). If you are in trouble, look to solve your retail issues first.

Be a Student of Success <u>and</u> Failure

Study other products/services not in your category that are successfully and unsuccessfully reaching your target, regardless of the type of product or service being sold. Automotive can learn from the quick-service restaurant (QSR), and salad dressing can study makeup to be more aware of its audience.

If the automotive industry had considered the price equals value messaging of QSR dollar menus, it might not have relied so heavily on cash-back incentives. Learning from other shopper experiences is a great tool when considering new ways to market products and services.

Manage Your Expectations and Set Reasonable Goals

A brand director from a dog food company wanted to increase and volume but was suffering from a decrease in distribution. If your product is not on the shelf, the best marketing strategy in the world can't help it. Instead of looking to sell more than what was there, the company had to look at what wants/needs/desires the product was meeting for the shopper, and set strategies that gave the sales force leverage with retailers. By delivering shopper benefit and through smart shopper-driven promotional efforts, the company was able to regain lost shelf space and eventually reach its sales and volume goals.

Be Retail-centric

If you want to reach your sales potential, it is critical to understand the retailer's shopper profile and corporate personality, and tailor plans accordingly.

- Know its goals/objectives before creating strategies for its stores.
- Adapt your plans to get better positioning in its environment.

Wal-Mart, the world's largest retailer, long ago discovered the value of its "retail-estate." Other retailers now understand they can push manufacturers to deliver exclusive marketing strategies that meet the needs of their specific customers. Without true partnership with key retailers, manufacturers could face missed opportunities and lost sales. This section will give examples of the changing tide in the retailer environment, and retailer demand for inclusion in product marketing plans.

Set Your Strategies By Key Retailers

Each retailer is a bit different from the next. Retailers' goals for their shoppers vary, as do their store layouts and shopper composition. Whereas it is much easier to execute one national promotion rather than five separate ones, retailers who believe you are partnering with them will make the extra effort and "exclusivity" worth your while in added exposure within the store environment.

It is crucial for sales and marketing to work together to set overall and specific strategies for success, and present those to the retailer.

Execute Research in the Competitive Retail Space

The experience of going to Disneyland is entirely different from having someone tell you what it's like. Attempting to set smart shopper strategies without retail immersion is incomplete at best.

Here's how you can improve your research in the retail environment:

- Form marketing and sales teams that regularly execute on-site visits at key retailers and report findings to the greater group.
- Rotate these teams so that all sales/marketing team members have a true understanding of the product's place within key retail environments throughout the year.
- Circulate weekly photos and reports of retail scenes with executive briefs highlighting what your brand and the competition are doing in the space.
- Study unrelated products that are succeeding in retail space (good placement, point-of-sale materials, etc.).
- Set full-size point-of-sale store schematics at corporate, including competition, to remind teammates of realness of retail.
- Send marketers out with sales force to get a real understanding of the sales environment and the POV of the retailer.

Shopper Retail-search Is Crucial

Shopper test where shoppers engage your product:

- Partner with key retailers to execute in-store intercepts and behavioral studies.
- Set up mobile on-site focus groups so that you can ask questions of shoppers while their purchase decision is fresh in their memory.

Limit the Amount of Questions You Ask

I know, this sounds crazy. However, focus groups often ask an hour's worth of questions about a three-second decision. The answers you need are often quite simple.

Why did you choose our product? Why did you choose the competitor's? What can we do to have you choose us? And how can we encourage you to choose more often?

Certainly, there are a host of other questions you can ask, but you risk overcomplicating the research and making the shoppers think well beyond what they really were thinking when they purchased the product or service.

Remember, a lion in her natural habitat acts differently from one in the zoo. Focus groups are helpful, but nothing comes close to getting the shopper in or as near to her retail environment as possible. Watch your shoppers to see how they engage with your product, competitive products, and ones outside of your category.

Sales and Marketing vs. Marketing for Sales

We've all seen a three-legged race. The team that can best adapt to each other always wins. Though a simple analogy, the same is true with sales and marketing forces. The better they join forces to succeed, the better their success at retail and the stronger their product will be.

A marketing team of a multimillion-dollar beverage product was convinced of its brand's strength, and relied on it primarily to sell products. According to the team, the top reason for their success was that they had always refused to lower their product's price. They were fooled by their own beliefs, caught up in an "it'll sell itself" mind-set. What the marketing team didn't realize was that the sales force and retailer were heavily discounting the product on the shelf. A separation of divisions leads to confusion and misconception, and can be dangerous to the brand's health.

Typically, marketing is concerned with brand value and sales is focused on price. And this, by no means, is the fault of the sales force. Retailers can vice grib hold the process, and the sales force does its best to make numbers. With that said, however, price does not absolutely equal value to all audiences, as most shoppers want a combination of both to feel good about their purchase decisions. Your shopper needs a reason to believe, and will believe what you teach them.

When McDonald's decided to sell its Big Mac® for ninety-nine cents and make the price the key point in its message to consumers, it guaranteed one thing for certain—it wouldn't be able to charge more than ninety-nine cents for a Big Mac easily again.

If you paint a "price equals value" message in the minds of shoppers, realize that it is difficult—and at times impossible—to reverse. Many players in the automotive industry found this out the hard way with cash-back incentives. By training shoppers to key in on cash-back incentives, car companies were forced to keep deeply discounting in order to meet the demands of the shoppers. Even though they would carry the message "for a limited time," they trained the shoppers to believe that the discounts were permanent.

Sales strategies and marketing strategies formed without cooperation can decimate a product. Typically, marketing groups concentrate on the brand first, advertising second, and its in-store message sometime after that. The sales force wants to sell, whatever way possible, so that they make their numbers. In truth, the marketing group must realize that their most important function is to sell more products/services, just as is the case for the sales force. The shared goal—the most important reason for either group to exist—makes it even more important for synergy between the two groups.

This section will suggest that "marketing sales" teams call on sales and marketing retailers together to find the best solutions to shopper-centric planning. Rather than having sidebar conversations, circling the wagons in the retail space will lead to more effective and efficient shopper-focused plans.

Developing "Shoppers First" Creative Strategies

Using Research and "Emotional Knowledge" to Guide Idea Generation

Regardless of What You're Doing, Start from the POV of Your Target Shoppers

It's imperative to realize that statistical information is not the same as knowing how it feels to be in the shopper's shoes. You can think you know simply because you're well-informed. The best creative comes from an intimate understanding, an "Emotional Knowledge," of the target audience.

Men and Women React Differently Because They're Wired Differently

One of the biggest mistakes made today in marketing is a lack of gender focus. Often, marketers will say, "Target is eighteen to forty-nine, male/female." There are rare instances where you'll find a fifty-fifty gender split among shoppers, so acting as if they're equally represented is dangerous and just plain silly.

In addition, thinking that an eighteen-year-old and a forty-nine–year-old are going to engage a product in the same way is a stretch. Figure out the sweet spot—the shopper segment that has the potential to buy the most product/service, and go from there. By saying you're going after everyone, you risk not getting anyone.

Becoming Shopper-centric

Remember: All Qualitative Marketing Research Is Imperfect

Marketers must weigh the strengths and weaknesses of various forms of research. Shopper focus groups, where shoppers are quizzed in a conference room by a moderator about their purchase habits, can be very informative, but are not perfect.

- Moderators and/or presentation materials can affect shopper responses.
- Shoppers don't give products an hour of their time when deciding at retail, so the deeper opportunity to consider their decision making within the probing of a focus group might not be accurate.
- Shoppers typically make their purchases alone, so the considerations of others in a focus group setting are counter to what they do in their natural habitat.
- The conference room isn't the aisle, and therefore not an exact environment. Because they're not in their purchase environment, their reactions may be skewed.
- Participants may say they are your shoppers, but might not be.
- Shoppers who might actually be the heavy users of a product might not attend focus groups away from retail.
- Often, focus group members want to please (thinking that if they don't, they will not get paid), and if they figure out what you're selling they might be more inclined to support your ideas.

It is critical to determine how much weight you place on the research you conduct. Shoppers aren't typically innovators. Whereas they would be more than willing to adopt a new offering at retail, proposing the same idea in a focus group setting might be too much change for them to consider.

Stay in Your Own Backyard

Arguably the most grievous error of the American Bar Association was the vote in the '70s to allow lawyers to advertise beyond small signs and an occasional mention in a church program. Once allowed only a small sign outside their office and an occasional advertisement in a church bulletin, lawyers decided that advertising could be executed successfully without damaging legal's fairly pristine reputation.

They left their own backyard, and before we knew it, became the litigious society we are today. Personal injury lawyers needed only to put a thirty-second ad on television to fill their coffers with lawsuits. "Hurt in an accident? Dial 1-800-INJURED and meet with a lawyer today at no cost to you!" In true shopper-centric camouflage, shoppers don't realize that these types of legal representatives typically only take the cases they can win easily, leaving those who have less-than-slam-dunk cases out in the legal cold.

Taking chances is important to marketing growth. Leaping into an abyss, however, should be avoided at all costs. Don't purport to be what you're not or do things you won't be proud of in the name of sales. Eventually, it will catch up to you.

Hire the Right Marketing Agency, and Trust It

Trust is a huge part of marketing. If you are the brand manager, be the brand manager. Marketing agencies draw on a wealth of experiences in a host of channels with hundreds of products when they look to create shopper-driven concepts for your product. Trust them. Brand managers who feel they need their ideas executed are wasting the time and the money they've spent on a marketing agency. This isn't to say that brand managers or CMOs or others aren't creative and innovative. Instead, it is simply about roles and responsibilities. The brand manager certainly knows the product best, but a smart, experienced marketing agency knows the shopper best, as it has sold that very shopper a host of other products/services in a myriad of areas beyond yours. A great agency will bring a lot of experience from many other channels. The philosophies used in selling paint can help you sell makeup, salad dressing, or cars. Letting good agencies do their jobs will make the process more efficient, effective, and less costly.

Understand the Retail-estates

One of the biggest mistakes marketers make is not focusing their attention on their key retail channels. If 70 percent of your volume is sold through Wal-Mart, it's important that a majority of your marketing focus is concentrated on Wal-Mart. This is not to say you ignore other retail accounts, but they should receive the attention equal to their percentage of importance to your business. You can and should identify growth areas, but be certain to spend relative to the opportunity.

Keep "Personal" Out of the Plan

Successful strategies focus foremost on the purchaser while keeping key retailer's goals/objectives in mind. Examples in this section may include a candy company brand manager who wanted to execute his idea that centered around divorce, the head of a cereal company who wanted to execute a program whereby children could send in-packed postcards to the homeless, and a vice president who told a marketing agency that *American Idol* was a ridiculous idea two years before his competition made millions from the property. In each case, a marketer's inability to get out of his own way endangered the product's retail success.

Fight for Simplicity

Shoppers don't sit in rooms, like we do, contemplating marketing strategies for weeks and months on end. It's been my experience that you know a good idea in the first second, and need not overthink it into blandness or complexity. Shoppers looking for bottled water, for example, see things simply. They haven't read the hundred pages of research. They haven't spent weeks debating how many beads of sweat should be dripping down the bottle in the display photo. They give about three seconds of attention to display, and decide if they are going to purchase. By debating and overthinking elements that are irrelevant to the shopper, time and money are wasted. The shoppers, and the three seconds they spend in front of a product display, determine retail success.

It's Not About the Sports Car

In an advertising agency conference room, an inexperienced yet passionate male creative suggested that a particular product, orange juice, needed to be "marketed like a sports car." While the group in the room found the notion to be exciting, the reality is that Mom doesn't see a sports car when she picks up the orange juice. She sees *orange juice*. The ad folks wanted to make something more exciting for themselves, without regard for the shopper. Cool and sexy is fine when you're selling beer or a Porsche®, but for most packaged goods you just need to be relevant and grounded.

The mom buying the orange juice just came from picking up her youngest at school. She has a limited amount of time to get her shopping done. Before racing home to make dinner, she has to get the kids to soccer practice. She is in front of the cold case, trying to make the best decision she can as quickly as possible.

If It's Working for the Shopper, Don't Get Rid of It

There's a misperception that if a marketing strategy has been executed before, it is somehow old and tired. Although the strategy might be mundane for the marketer who wants to try something new, it might still be motivating to the shopper.

Certainly, there are exceptions to overuse, but the key is to understand whether or not the idea is still compelling to the shopper. Yoplait hasn't left lids. McDonald's still plays Monopoly. There's no need to change what works. In fact, successful initiatives often stay in the shoppers' memories, making it unnecessary to spend as much to inform the shoppers as you did in the first iteration.

Know When to Stand Alone and When to Borrow

The only major sponsorships a manufacturer should consider are those that will deliver more opportunity for sales, not simply awareness. Further, all members of key retail teams should be queried about a potential sponsorship to gauge their interest before a contract is signed. Successful sponsorships are first and foremost engaging to the shopper, thereby lifting sales at retail. Keep in mind, however, that the retailer owns the real estate and it is important to have alignment whenever possible.

To illustrate, one major general merchandise retailer got wind of a multimillion-dollar deal struck between a movie studio and a consumer products giant. The retailer was responsible for most of the manufacturer's sales, and was irate that the company would cut a deal without asking the retailer if its stores were willing to support the sponsorship. The retailer threatened to accept only product that didn't carry any reference to the entertainment partnership. The retailer wanted to make sure that the offerings were right for its shopper, and wanted to be valued for the exposure provided to the packaged goods company within the retail environment.

This section will also explore the difference in perception between a brand manager's quest for "ownability" and the shopper POV regarding borrowed equity and sponsorship use.

Seek Out Alternate Means of Exposure

Jaguar® ran an innovative test-drive program with select W Hotels®, giving the car company a means of exposure outside its showrooms. W Hotel guests had the opportunity to use the cars, essentially becoming willing test-drive participants. By searching out other products and services targeting the same audience, companies can break through messaging clutter in new and unique ways. Within the store environment, partnering with a complementary product can drive sales while giving the product another area in the store where it can sell. Putting cookies next to the milk in the cold case suggestive sells the pairing and gives both more opportunity for sales.

Partnerships with a like-minded product can help products create news in alternate avenues, provide opportunities with product/service engagement, and increase sales.

Be Cautious of the Slippery Slope of Price Equals Value Messaging

It would seem that low price would be the perfect shopper-centric message, but that isn't often the case. If shoppers were only looking the lowest price, they would choose the lowest-priced item in every category. If price were the only factor, they wouldn't care about quality or added-value incentives.

Price equals value is a slippery slope for manufacturers and retailers, and it's not necessary from a shopper-centric point of view. Wal-Mart's retailtainment strategy shows how the world's leading discounter believes it is not all about "always low prices." Research shows that shoppers want an experience that goes beyond price, and no retailer can have the lowest prices all the time on every product in the store.

The leading retailer's price match guarantee is a savvy move for the price-sensitive shopper. It paints a picture in the minds of shoppers that Wal-Mart has the lowest prices. Knowing that a minority of shoppers will bring competitive advertisements into the store and price check works in the store's favor. Further, thousands of items are exclusive to Wal-Mart, making price checking a moot point. It is a win for Wal-Mart and gives shoppers something they want—the feeling that they're making the right purchase decisions.

Less profit also can mean less money for innovation, added value, or a more engaging retail presence. It's dangerous to go simply on price when you're trying to make the type of new news in the purchase environment that will grab a shopper's attention and get the retailer to back your programs.

Look to Make Negatives Into Positives for the Shopper

> "We searched for the naked truth, got down to the bare facts, and she kind of caught us with our pants down," said Southwest Airlines Chief Executive Officer Gary Kelly, apologizing to a scantily clad, buxom young female customer who was allowed to stay on a flight only after wrapping herself in a blanket. (This is more than the usual Southwest humor. It's the CEO sending the message that the famed corporate culture created by former CEO Herb Kelleher lives on and will be embraced even as the airline struggles with a changing environment, rising costs and possible changes in its business model. Southwest then milked the story, adding "The story has great legs," and launched an ad campaign poking fun at themselves, saying "People are saying we've gone from hot pants to hot flashes!" and rolling out a "mini skirt promotion" for fares.) The Dallas Morning News, "Southwest says 'Sorry' for Objection to Woman's Attire," Sept. 14, 2007

Southwest initially received damaging press regarding this incident, but through smart marketing strategies turned it completely around. The airline gave discounts to women in miniskirts, and even allowed flight attendants to play along. It was a brilliant shopper apology and a shopper-centric promotion that was fully in keeping with their image.

When Yoplait executed the breast cancer lids promotion, industry leaders were in disbelief that any product would dare associate its brand with cancer. Surely, you didn't want someone to think of your brand and cancer—that would kill the image! Yoplait understood the wants/needs/desires of the shopper and put her first. The rest is sales success history, and a program that has become a mainstay for the brand. Yoplait lids and the Susan G. Komen partnership is a textbook shopper-centric initiative.

This section delves into the importance of reaction to shopper negatives (whether it be with your product or in his/her lives) to increase sales.

Making Your Mark vs. Making It Matter

If you intend to stay with a company for twenty years, you might look at how you create, deliver, and gauge the success of your marketing strategies. Unfortunately, average corporate employment in marketing departments has declined significantly. More than ever, many marketers are looking to create big news quickly so they can make the next great job jump. However, this isn't always what's best for the shopper or the best dollar spend for the company.

Try to make a program that matters to the shopper, and you'll make your mark by increasing sales. If you try to simply make your mark, without a sales focus, your program won't matter.

This section highlights the change in corporate America, and the effect it has on companies, agencies, and shoppers in terms of marketing.

Constructing Your Shopper-centric Plan

Know Your Shopper

Execute various forms of legitimate research in-store with real shoppers in their environment. Don't rely on focus groups for all your answers.

Investigate

What draws shoppers to your product's area of the store? What percentage of shelf space do you have? How are you competing on price/value/promotional offers with your competition?

Know the Retail-estate

Figure out what your niche can be in the retail-estate you have or don't have.

Partner with Your Key Retailers

Meet with the retailers to discuss their goals/objectives. Ask to meet with the retailer's marketing group, not only the sales group.

Seek Out Competitive Success and Failure

See how your competition is doing it better, or how it is failing, and learn from both.

Form a Sales/Marketing Cooperative

Avoid sidebar conversations. Instead, circle the wagons. Get your sales and marketing teams together and find ways to take the journey together.

Win the Space Race

Decide how you can win the space at retail by delivering more of what the shopper wants/needs/desires.

Make Your Knowledge Work

After you've identified your shopper and understand your key retailers, devise your marketing strategy.

Create!

Deliver clear, concise creative messaging to the in-store environment that excites the retailer and prompts your shopper to purchase the product. Let your innovators innovate! Let creatives create! You will win at the register.

Develop Your Advertising

Once you've decided your strategic brand/product plan, look at how to make it come to life in your advertising. Realize that your consumer and shopper may be different, and plan accordingly. Running ads on Sport Center® when your shopper is female might not work. Find your audience and give them a compelling reason to remember you.

Regroup with Key Retailers

Meet with key retailers again to show your plans, and make certain that you will have the opportunity to participate during their key shopper initiatives.

Execute the Program

Get the sales and marketing groups together and share the responsibility of the execution.

Research In-store to See How Shoppers Are Engaging Your Program

This will be one of the best ways to find out why shoppers engaged, or avoided.

Hold a Program Postmortem

Execute purchaser-focused back-end analysis. Involve retailer, sales force, and actual purchasers who did or didn't choose to buy your product.

"And Now a Word from Our Moral Compass…"

Don't Forget the Ethos

Although it may not seem to have an obvious plank in the platform of shopper-centrics, ethics are crucial to executing effective work the right way. And, much like missteps in the brand love dance, a lack of ethics has, in the past, thrown the industry off its rhythm. No example is more evident in recent years than the business of pitching new business.

"Just because you can," an old boss warned, "doesn't make it right." Just because a corporation can invite (read "force") three to five marketing agencies into a pitching war over and over again for every single project doesn't make it right. In fact, it's surprisingly bad for business. (For those unfamiliar with the process, a new business pitch is a work assignment the client requests from selected agencies. It contains research, strategy, and creative work, for which the agencies are typically paid at a loss or receive no money at all.)

In recent years, many brand marketers seemed to have decided that having three to five agencies fighting it out for every project was a good idea. At face value, this might seem to make sense. After all, if the agencies are willing to do it, what's the harm? You'll get three to five different answers to your marketing challenge, and you'll get to cherry-pick the best one every time you host a pitch. (If these same brand marketers had to pitch for their jobs against three others every three to six months, they might think about it differently—but I digress.) It's the equivalent to ordering four entrees at a restaurant, trying them all, and sending three (or maybe even all four) back, and doing that every time you feel like going out for a really expensive dinner.

Now, this is not to say that pitching or competition is bad. In fact, most agencies look forward to showcasing their expertise and winning a new client. The problem is, many brands have become addicted to the pitch and no longer award agency of record (permanent status) to one agency. Instead, they invite agencies again and again to pitch every project that the client needs to fill a marketing calendar. This costs thousands of dollars to agencies every year, and because of a lack of commitment by the client it stretches agency personnel thin as they attempt to cover non-revenue-generating projects. A typical marketing agency can enter twenty or so pitches a year, at thousands of dollars per pitch in hard costs, travel, and personnel hours.

If we look past how—in some instances—ruthless it is to put competent agencies in a permanent and costly pitch mode, we can consider the disservice done to the product's marketing. Corporations benefit immensely from strong agency partnerships. When working correctly, the synergy between agency and corporation makes for a seamless, organic working process. Further, agencies that are secure in their position with a client have the opportunity to staff correctly for the business volume, adding to the efficiency and effectiveness of the process. Most importantly, creative and account persons alike from the agency will have the opportunity to learn about the company and its products inside and out, greatly reducing the learning curve and margin of error over time.

The responsibility between agency and client is two-pronged. The agency has a responsibility to the client to deliver great work honestly and with integrity. The client has the responsibility to treat the agency with respect, and within the constructs of fairness. Both sides must hold themselves to the highest ethical standards.

Just because you can doesn't make it right. Speaking as someone who has worked on both the client and agency sides of marketing, doing what's right best serves your business and your sales.

ARTICLES

The following are articles Ms. O'Leary has published on *The Huffington Post* and in various marketing publications.

Sadly, There's No MBA for Imagination

There are some indisputable facts in our glorious world. Men can't give birth. You can't cheat death. And you can't educate your way to creativity.

Northwestern University's prestigious Kellogg Business School doesn't have an MBA program that teaches people how to see what's not yet there. Harvard can't coach its highly intelligent student body on how to become imaginative. You can ask people to think outside boxes, but the mere question should tell you the shape you're in.

In many marketing circles, the client's education has become a hazard bigger than the sand traps on the golf courses that used to define the business elite. More than a few "B-schools" have fostered a false sense of deity among their student bodies, and the danger is that rice paper on the wall is becoming a more powerful driver than the gifts of imagination, innovation, and creativity.

Traditional "creatives" don't typically get MBAs, because education beyond the basic tools of the trade (art and writing) has long been considered damaging to one's imagination. (You don't want to be "boxed" in by unnecessary parameters and case studies of others' work and numbers when you think. You want to have as unfettered a path as possible.) And yet, creative ideas must fight their way through the sea of formally educated minds in order to see the light of day. Pushing creative ideas through people who aren't creative is a massive feat, especially given the layers of bureaucracy in corporate America today.

Innovative minds rarely talk about their formal education, unless it's to joke about their failure within it. Historically, great creative minds often bomb as students of others' thinking. Instead, *innovators like to hang their hats on ideas, not ideology*. And that's the big difference.

Sam Walton, grand innovator that he was, wouldn't get hired at Wal-Mart corporate today. Ray Kroc, the hustling milkshake salesman who never attended college, wouldn't find a place for his box-less thinking at today's McDonald's. Willy Wonka, if he had existed, never would have made it inside the hallowed halls of Hershey's® simply because of the creative way he dressed.

There was a time that the MBA was simply an extension of the golf course boys club. It proved to be an efficient way to pass over candidates who didn't have one without seeming discriminatory. It wasn't because a pass over was female or minority or old or didn't swim in the right social circles, but that he/she didn't have a piece of paper that said he/she was properly trained. It was a convenient filter to keep the club in good standing. But a superior course load does not build creativity and great ideas are not reserved for the educated. The mind either has it, or it doesn't.

When players and coaches witness natural skills on the playing field, they'll quip, "Hey, ya can't teach that." So it is with imagination. It is a gift, a way of viewing the world that is manna from heaven. Some people are great with numbers, some with science, some with analysis. And then there are the rare among us who can create new ideas in business, and in particular marketing, which engage shoppers and motivate them to take specific sales-driving actions.

One of the saddest trends in marketing today is agency "death by marketing department." This occurs when the marketing department of a corporation overrules its agencies time and time again, opting for its own ideas instead and turning agency creative minds into hand servants of the marketing department's work. And then, when the multi-million-dollar initiatives fail to perform, the brand manager fires the ad agency because the spots didn't work and the marketing agency because sales were flat. Agencies have moved more and more into a vendor rather than partner relationship. In the end, this power shift compromises imaginative solutions and endangers brand success.

Creativity is a gifted way of thinking; an art, not a science. It cannot be birthed from pie charts and graphs and analysis. It looks simply at the people it's trying to reach and figures out a way to reach them. What is Suzie Shopper's want/need/desire? What innovation will get her attention? Motivate her to take action? Make her feel good about her decision? It's often said that "a good idea can come from anywhere." Yes, it's true. But a good idea can't come out of thin air. It's the massive exception, not the rule, when an uncreative mind hits pay dirt.

In today's marketplace, where competition for the shopper's attention has never been greater, one might ask, "What would Sam Walton do?" Simple. He would search out the innovators—not necessarily the ones with rice paper on the wall. Advanced educations are outstanding business assets, he'd agree, but creativity and innovation can't be learned in a classroom.

The Marketing Genius of Erectile Dysfunction

We must tip our hats to the creative and strategic geniuses among us who took one of the most embarrassing maladies literally known to man and made it sexy. Erectile Dysfunction (ED) has gone from eunuch-forming to brawn-building. Not only can men have ED, but they can look more virile than ever on classy TV spots with attractive women in their age brackets after they've rectified it.

Ad agencies the world over used to rely on before and after shots to show successful medication use. We were the "sneeze with a red nose and watery eyes to show the common cold" and "smile under sunshine to show relief from it" industry. Yet in the case of ED, this formula presented a unique set of issues. (Certainly, before or after shots would not be thought of highly by the FCC, FTC, or network executives.) Thanks to Pfizer's Viagra ad agency and others, we've profited by putting a positive spin on what was once considered verboten and humiliating. Instead of showing suffering, we've successfully shown the emotional benefits of medicinal solution. And in the process, we took what was once a shamed population and made it stand tall once more.

ED has taught us that positive mind-set advertising can change consumers' perception of the things that embarrass them most. And therein lies an even bigger opportunity. What if we were to identify other maligned conditions and make them acceptable?

Taking a page out of the ED playbook, the mental health industry could grow by the billions of dollars. Make it okay to have a mental issue and a sign of strength to want to get better, and corporations and therapists the world over will profit.

TV commercials for depression drugs show depressed people feeling wildly depressed. Depressed people already know how bad they feel. Why not show them happy and well? Proud that they are no longer depressed? Living full and complete lives? We didn't show men suffering in the bedroom from ED, so why make depression sufferers, who already feel bad, feel worse and more ashamed of their illnesses? Pharmaceutical companies can learn a lesson from ED and begin to sell a host of medications that deliver on the hope of mental wellness.

The opportunity may be even greater in the realm of therapeutic services, but a monumental shift in ideology will be necessary. The AMA, ADA, and ABA have allowed their members to advertise (with varying forms of regulation) for years. Yet the vast majority of psychological associations and licensing boards allow for no solicitation of any kind. In the United States, you can advertise various ways to sedate one's self with a host of adult beverages, but it is unacceptable to let those looking for mental health know that services to help them exist. Given the billion dollars consumers spend on the outside of themselves every year, basic logic would lead us to believe people would be willing to spend on the inside as well. Talk therapy, group, and in-patient facilities all stand to benefit.

If Viagra is any indication, the righting of the mental health ship begins a change in perception, championed by advertising. If we can convince potential consumers that it's not only all okay but a wonderfully strong sign of moral fiber to work on one's gray matter, we'll help create the next multibillion-dollar marketing opportunity.

Want to Sell? Know the Retail-estate

Ask most marketers about business, and they'll tell you about their brands.

They'll show you the latest ad campaign or mention the celebrity endorser they've signed or bowl game sponsored or groundbreaking guerrilla marketing effort soon to be executed. There would be talk of media buys and awareness and penetration and Q scores. Marketing strategies and promotions might be mentioned in terms of "spikes" and key drive periods. And, if asked, they'll share a myriad of models, graphs, and data points about their brands' core consumers.

Certainly, consumer products marketers should be able to wow you with reams of data that explain the peaks and valleys of the yearly cycle. There are growth areas and shopper acquisition issues and retention challenges to consider. There are lost share and increased volume and a host of other things that captivate us or are so shotgun detailed that they simply dumbfound.

But where the rubber meets the proverbial road, the place where all these numbers come from, is in an aisle in a brick-and-mortar retail space that Susie Shopper frequents—far from a corporate campus or agency conference room where brand marketing is born.

Rather than delving into a comprehensive "where" and "who" understanding of the purchase cycle, marketers and their brand agencies often prefer to talk about the product or service. Why? Maybe because it's the part the manufacturer owns and therefore can control. The company produces the brand. The marketers create its image, one that is hopefully "ownable" in its uniqueness. There's typically a deep sense of pride in brand creation, and marketers tend to attach themselves to it with the suction power of a remora. The brand is a part of corporate pride, and therefore stands as what is most important in the minds of the marketing department and its agencies.

Truth be told, our emphasis can be misplaced. The most important entity within any marketing construct is the shopper. She, in fact, owns the brand because she is the one who purchases it. (The first rule of marketing existentialism is that no brand has a value until it is purchased.) The next critical cog in the marketing wheel is the retailer. The retailer owns the environment—the "retail-estate," if you will—where the shopper purchases the product. In almost all circumstances, the retailer has the final say in terms of the overall messaging and offerings that are made to its shopper. First and foremost, the consumer products marketer must understand the wants/needs/desires of the retailer and its key shopper in order to sell the most products possible in an efficient and cost-effective way. Whereas the product and its image are obviously wildly important, they are valueless if they don't meet certain criteria in the minds of shoppers and retailers.

When brands begin to slip, often manufacturers look to reinvent, revamp, and/or relaunch the brand rather than explore new efforts at retail. Why? Maybe it seems like a catastrophic change such as rebranding is what is necessary to stop a slide. Maybe because it seems like the easiest way to make a big bang. Sometimes it's to make a mark, leave a mark, or in rare instances out of boredom. Maybe sometimes it's just because it's easier than other options. Partnering with key retailers is time/work intensive and mired in its own complexities, but when performed successfully pays big dividends. Learning where your shopper and your key retailer's shopper intersect is essential to efficient and cost-effective marketing.

Let's face it: designing account-specific marketing programs for key general merchandise, grocery, drug, and department stores and other shopper sales environments isn't typically the exciting part of marketing. Most marketing heads and ad men dream about shooting the killer TV spot on a beach in South Africa, not brainstorming the best way to get a detergent center stage on Wal-Mart's Action Alley. But the sales war can't be won simply by creating a great brand image. The victory is secured every time a shopper pulls her credit card out of her wallet and shoots it through the scanner at checkout.

If you represent a consumer products company that doesn't own its retail space, every game you play is an away game. You need to know all the ins and outs of the fields of play before constructing your game plans. You need a deep understanding of each arena's officials and players, even the ones on the sidelines. The game doesn't happen on your practice field or in unrelated pregame rituals or on the pep bus. It's won or lost once the ball is put into play, real contact is made, and everyone sees what you're made of.

Marketing in Disguise

The primary job of marketing is to promote sales, and those in the industry use a myriad of tactics to entice shoppers to action. Advertising, direct mail, sales promotion, and PR experts have a host of persuasive armament in their arsenals. When we communicate a meaningful message that delivers on the wants/needs/desires of the shopper, sales increase.

However, the manner in which marketers put the carrot in front of the shopper isn't always black and white. Certainly, we know not every shopper will take advantage of every offer presented. Yet, when we knowingly play in the darker parts of the gray to drive sales, we're doing a disservice to the shopper and the industry. A good deal is not a good deal when marketers misinform shoppers and/or misrepresent offers.

Here are just a few examples:

The Nearly If Not Impossible Mail-in Rebate

The mail-in rebate began with the best of intentions. A retailer might not have wanted to drop the price of a product, for example, but the manufacturer wanted to give something back on the price to reward the shopper. The engaged shopper viewed the enticement positively, and took action. Many present-day rebates, unfortunately, have become art forms of complication rather than real rewards.

Some marketers design rebate offers that generate sales while making redemption nearly impossible. We want to be able to say shoppers can get one hundred dollars back on a new printer because that might be just the right enticement, but we don't want them to actually do it. The reason for purchase and the reality of reward make for an unsuccessful shopper experience. There has been and always will be a place for the mail-in rebate as a marketing tactic. However, no rebate should be executed with shopper deception in its crosshairs.

Sadly, sometimes the shopper doesn't even know he or she is being rebated. A hotel chain offered a "lowest price guarantee" on its Web site. When I found a lower price on another Web site, I called the frequent traveler 800 number and asked why the price on the hotel's site wasn't the lowest. I was told to book the stay on the hotel's Web site at the higher price and pay for it at the higher price. Within twenty-four hours of check-in, I needed to download a form from the site and submit it with documentation of the lower price I found on the competitive site. (Note: not many travelers hit the road with their laptops and printers.)

After hotel corporate received and verified the documentation, the shopper would be rebated the difference and given a fifty-dollar gift card that was only redeemable at the hotel. As a marketer, I would guess the number of shoppers who take advantage of the offer and actually get the lowest price is less than 0.5 percent. The offer is framed so that the hotel can advertise a guarantee that it created in hopes that shoppers would simply believe the guarantee. Further, it counted on those shoppers who checked the guarantee not going through the trouble of taking advantage of it. Rebates, in whatever form, should be attainable to shoppers without unnecessary effort. Otherwise, marketers are designing to deceive.

Product Downsizing

"We don't need to raise prices, let's just make the product smaller!" Certainly, from a profit perspective, this might be a necessary evil in some instances. Realize, however, that Suzie Shopper knows you're doing it, and you might risk her wrath. Price does not solely equal value. Price plus quality plus product usage (size fits into this) equals value.

Within the realm of product downsizing lives the serving size sleight of hand. Anyone who has read the side of a regular soda or a cereal box knows how marketers try to make products seem more appealing. The soda is only 110 calories, provided you only drink half of the single-serve bottle. The can of soup contains only eight grams of fat, provided you leave half of it in the can. Amazingly, the bag of potato chips you put in the cart has enough individual servings for a family of twenty. Serving size reality as well as nutritional information should be considered by government regulators.

No Supply and Lots of Demand

Try as it might, the government can't watch over every retailer in the country advertising a steal on a new flat screen TV or a killer deal on an entry-level car.

My brother once worked at a car dealership. The sales force was told that if anyone sold the lowest-priced car (there was only one, and it was carried in all its advertising), he or she would be fired on the spot. The dealership banked on the salesman's ability to up-sell the shoppers into higher-priced vehicles. When the bait is nonexistent and the switch to another product is planned, it is unethical and often illegal. Yes, products sell out. Yes, the objective is to sell products and services. However, if a shopper is lured into a store for a deal that the retailer knows is nonexistent for all intents and purposes, the retailer puts shopper trust (along with its own ethos) in jeopardy.

The good Lord himself wouldn't have the credit rating necessary to take advantage of 99.9 percent of the automotive offers we've seen on TV. "Two thousand dollars cash back and no money down for qualified buyers!" is the ultimate offer bait and switch. Get the shoppers into the showroom, get them interested, and then eventually tell them they can't have the deal that drove them to the dealership in the first place. Certainly, when applying for credit, those with higher scores deserve better pricing, as they are less of a risk. However, touting an offer that almost no one can take advantage of as though it was the answer for the masses should not be legally allowed.

The Unseen Add-ons

Frequent fliers amass airline miles that may be redeemed for free travel. If you're lucky enough to find the flights you need available for use with your reward, most airlines require you to pay them upwards of two hundred dollars to use the miles for the "free travel" you've earned as part of a "service fee."

"Plus shipping and handling" has been a mainstay since the '70s, flying quietly below the government's radar. That amazing knife set is only "five dollars—a fifty-dollar value!", plus shipping and handling. What's shipping and handling? Well, shoppers can find that out when they call or go online to order the product. In truth, the knife set is not five dollars. Not even close.

Full price disclosure should be required by law, and not accepted as a surprise add-on a shopper finds out after engaging in the purchase process.

Unlike the American Medical Association or the American Bar Association or other self-governing bodies, the various marketing associations (AAAA, AMA, etc.) cannot disbar or cancel the certification of marketers. The vast majority of those in the industry are committed to the integrity of their work and the honesty of their efforts. However, the few who are not ethical taint our industry. Those playing by the rules are harmed by those who are not, and typically are in support of fair regulation in areas where the government can intercede. In the areas outside of government intervention, however, it is up to marketers to self-govern. If we want to believe, we must be fervent in our commitment to consistently telling a more perfect truth.

Overthinking to Stinking: The Dangers of Overly Complicated Marketing

Since the beginning of ad time, marketers sold salad dressing. Today, we still sell salad dressing. The two most important constants of Shopper Mom haven't wavered: she's still a mom, and she's still trying to make the best decisions for her family. She might have worked then, and probably does now. "Go play outside" has morphed into playgroups and play dates. Technology has had an impact on her family's life, but isn't really a factor when she's pushing a cart down the aisle of her grocery store. The retail environment has changed, albeit not drastically. Stores still sell products, and she still buys for her family.

The basics of Shopper Mom haven't become more complex, but our attempts at reaching her have grown substantially. In today's marketing world, seemingly endless cadres of marketing personnel at corporate and its agencies often spend countless hours poring over a marketing solution for a product before Mom can pick it from the shelf. Marketing solutions are often created by committee and agreed to by quorum. In the '70s we had research, but our logic and intuition and common sense drove us. Now, reams of analysis and formulas and equations and modules and charts of all shapes and sizes complicate the jobs we do. And, in most instances, the overabundance is unnecessary, as it is neither time- nor cost-effective.

Overthinking to Stinking: The Dangers of Overly Complicated Marketing

A unique marketing idea is like a rock on the side of a riverbank. It has flat spots and rough spots and points and dips and crags and a host of things that make it different from the rest. Walk into the river a few steps, and you'll find water-polished stones. They are more similar to one another than different. Too much interaction with the water has softened them into commonness. When you want the best creative idea, you need to allow the rocks their uniqueness. By complicating the marketing process with too much input of both human and data forms, we risk polishing the rock beyond effectiveness and waste time and money in our process.

For most consumer products sold at retail, marketers don't need the complications that we feel make us smarter. When considering creative concept generation, there's an easy way for you to test the theory. Let's say chewy granola bars are our product, and the time frame is back to school. Target is Mom for kids. Give the assignment to a strong two-person creative team. Give them a week to come up with three or four concepts. (You only need one winning idea, so coming up with twenty ideas is a waste of time and effort.) Now, create reams of research and data of all shapes/sizes about Mom and kids and back to school and granola bars and lunch boxes and snacking occasions, and brief a second team. Let that team consist of as many talented people as you can find, and make sure that all are motivated to participate. Give Team 2 a month to solve the challenge.

When Team 2 is finished, regroup. Both teams will have logical, creative solutions that meet the goals/objectives of the challenge. Both teams will have ideas that will deliver motivation to Shopper Mom and increase sales during the promotional period. The difference? You'll have spent thousands of dollars and countless hours of time and effort on the second, more complicated effort. Further, because there were fewer cooks in the kitchen, the small group will probably deliver even better creative than the much larger team. The majority of great ideas in our industry didn't come from a series of committees armed with a plethora of charts and graphs and a host of opinions. They came from a handful of creative thinkers who possessed a fair balance of fact and gray matter. Overthinking isn't a formula for success, but for failure.

Creative "brainstorms," groups of marketers sitting in a room pondering creative solutions for marketing challenges, are valuable tools, provided the persons assembled are creative thinkers and the manner in which the group is hosted is valuable. It's when/where they are used in a creative process that should be considered carefully. When I began in the '80s in marketing, a two-person creative team would get a two-page assignment and be sent on its way to come up with ideas. That was our job, after all, as creatives working for a marketing agency. After the ideas were in concept form (a program theme and a brief description, often in three or four bullet points), we regrouped with creative supervisors. If we didn't think we had the winning ideas yet, we held a brainstorm with other creative thinkers. When the creative group was satisfied, we brought the ideas to the account team and then to the client. The process used to create ideas thirty years ago worked. It just cost the client a lot less money.

As an industry, we need to trust ourselves like we once did, and we need to begrudgingly accept failure. We need to trust our instincts without committees and over-the-top attempts to make fact out of our guesses through inordinate amounts of analysis. We have to realize that even the best guesses at times miss the mark. Overthinking doesn't make an idea stronger, and might have the exact opposite effect. There are no guarantees in what we do, and feeling that stacking the deck involves beating dead horses gives us a feigned sense of security. Ray Kroc didn't have a committee when he met the McDonald brothers. He just had an idea. Big thinking doesn't need to be complex, it simply needs a logical soul designed to drive sales.

Shopper Mom's wants/needs/desires haven't changed a lot in the past thirty or so years. She still stands in front of the salad dressing, and still has a choice to make. She has not inundated the process with opinion or information, we have. At the end of the day, she's going to buy Wishbone®, or she's not. We're the ones that need to persuade her effectively and efficiently.

We can all learn a lesson from Shopper Mom. She doesn't go out of her way to waste time and money, and neither should we.

Crowdsourcing: A Legitimate Marketing Resource

At the risk of committing industry blasphemy, marketers aren't the only ones with great ideas. Just log on to YouTube, MySpace, Facebook, or a host of other consumer- generated content sites and you'll soon realize that people can be immensely creative without having it as a descriptor on their business cards.

I firmly believe that a properly directed creative mind can sell just about anything in any category in any retail environment. Further, great ideas can come from a variety of places, regardless of formal training. My first boss, marketing patriarch Bud Frankel, believed that anyone could contribute creatively. It made no difference to him if you were the lead creative or the guy pushing the mail cart. A good idea is just that. (Mr. Frankel's ability to promote creativity in the most likely and unlikely of places was one of the things that made him the best to have ever played the game.)

There were more than a few ad agencies quaking in their respective boots by the trend of consumer-generated brand campaigns. The Doritos "Crash the Super Bowl" TV commercial contest and others like it proved that consumers had something to say about the brands they or their shoppers' chose, and had the creative talent necessary to tell a compelling story. Realizing that an audience's creative energy could be harnessed to increase awareness, engagement, and sales, marketers in certain rabid fan categories have given even more control of the brand to consumers. Mountain Dew's current "Fans Take Over the Brand" campaign, Dewmocracy, challenges consumers to create everything from new product flavors to marketing strategies, ending in a vote by fans to determine the next new product introduction.

A lover of terms beyond measure, the marketing industry looked to label the consumer content trend. First we called it consumer- or user-generated, then landed for a time on "open source" marketing, which came from the tech world where outside programmers collaborated to create platforms. Jeff Howe coined the term *crowdsourcing* in 2006, defining it as "the process by which the power of the many can be leveraged to accomplish feats that were once the province of the specialized few." Today, crowdsourcing has morphed into an industry, where firms invite and reward outside participants to tackle creative brand challenges.

I was recently introduced to BigHeads Network, a firm that's taken a slightly more evolutionary approach to crowdsourcing. Instead of limiting its participants to creative minds who hail from the marketing world or simply members of the target audience, BigHeads accesses a diverse group of minds with different perspectives to drive new idea generation. The company amassed over one thousand minds from a myriad of disciplines (entertainment, health care, sports, technology, politics, education, fashion, etc.) to generate product innovations and marketing solutions.

In one such instance, a cosmetics company was looking to improve female consumers' engagement with its foundation product. BigHeads challenged certain members of its brain trust to generate ideas and inspiration: a Navy SEAL who used camouflage to blend into surroundings, a woman who studied reptiles that changed color for safety, and a car restoration guru who used tools to match paint on old vehicles. Although they weren't customers, marketers, or researchers, they had deep insights into the exact issue and brought truly innovative solutions to the table.

Beyond crowd selection, the questions posed to the brain trust are critically important pieces of the crowdsource equation. The firm must ask the right questions of its network to give the thinkers the best opportunity for success, and must be careful to direct the process without influencing the outcome. This is the secret sauce of a good crowdsourcing company, as asking the right questions at the right time to the right people is the fuel for this type of innovation. Lastly, how a crowdsource firm reads and packages the data can make or break the effort.

Crowdsourcing has proven itself as a legitimate player in the areas of marketing insight and innovation. It is, however, a complement to rather than a replacement of the role agencies play in the marketing of consumer goods and services. The ability to be creative is a gift, and strong agencies successfully corral the gifts, skills, and experience of many to grow brands.

To all the agencies out there still trembling over consumer-generated marketing efforts, fear not (or at least, fear less). There will always be a place for big marketing minds within the hallowed halls of corporate America. It's just that now you might be sitting next to a crowd.

Thanks to Spam, It's Not Junk Mail Anymore

Like a shiny new bike at Christmas, marketers in the '90s fell hopelessly in love with the newfangled promise of e-mail. We marveled at all the ways we could use it reach millions of shoppers at light speed while gleefully avoiding postage and printing costs. What could be better?

But alas, no marketing good lasts forever. Our industrial lust for direct e-mail eventually turned against us. We created a dread-filled word—*spam*—to describe our overzealousness. E-mail hosts created spam filters and spam folders to keep our messaging away from our inboxes. Audiences quickly disarmed the "You've Got Mail" computer voice, as the mountains of spam would have led them to insanity.

As marketers, we had to begrudgingly admit a simple fact: if we sent our brand's message to people who didn't want to hear it or didn't like the way we were presenting it or didn't want to hear it with the frequency we thought acceptable, we were doing ourselves more harm than good. Efficiency without effectiveness is waste, and frustrated and/or overburdened shoppers and/or consumers won't buy what we're selling.

Elder statespersons of the industry (anyone over the age of forty) might fondly remember the low-tech precursor to e-mail marketing: traditional or "snail" mail. When done properly (the right message to the right shopper at the right time), it was an extremely effective way to reach audiences. People didn't get a lot of mail back in the olden days, so the chances that they'd read it over their morning cup of Joe were pretty high. For a myriad of companies, it was an effective way to target shoppers for typically a lot less cash than traditional advertising.

Before the sun rose on the Internet and QVC and infomercials, mail was the mainstay of direct to shopper communication. Mailings could be targeted by zip code, giving marketers the opportunity to hit specific geographical areas and demographics. Many marketers promoting high-end products, from Cartier to cars to cruises, found it to be a good way to convey a deeper sell message than was possible in a print ad or a thirty-second spot. The low-end bill-stuffer crowd, selling everything from off-brand dish soap to cat beds to personalized checks, also found the medium worthwhile. Yet the unfortunate result of marketers' efforts, as we all now know, was a mailbox overflowing with often less-than-valued information.

Americans voiced their opposition to inundation, and the term *junk mail* was born. Millions would toss rather than tear open, making many direct mail messages worthless. (A man in New England famously heated his home by burning his junk mail, becoming one of the very first direct mail recyclers.)

Savvy marketers did their level best to fight through clutter and make direct mail work for appropriate products/services. We improved our strategies, creating messages in envelopes and packages and postcards that stood out in the mailbox crowd. Still, it proved to be more time-consuming and expensive and dramatically less flexible than the Internet's e-mail capabilities. In short, the payoff wasn't worth the fight.

At the onset of e-mail, in large part because of the newness of the medium and the small number of e-mails received, people opened the messages and read them. Once it crossed the threshold into the dreaded land of spam, driven in large part by the underbelly of sellers hocking everything from prescription drugs from Canada to male enhancement devices to stock tips, promotional e-mail became much less effective. For legitimate marketers selling products/services who sent an abundance of "blasts" to their databases, the damage often caused was oversell. Without fully considering frequency of purchase and how it affects the shopper's interest in hearing a particular message, marketers let the ease and convenience get away from them. Internet users, tired of intrusion, began to throw out marketing babies with their Internet bath water.

Often when kids get new toys for Christmas, they forget about the old toys they knew and loved. Open just about any mailbox in America and you'll hear a faint cavernous echo and discover a marketer's dream environment. With fewer companies choosing traditional direct mail, consumers are more amused by it than turned off. Consumers are more apt to open than to toss or burn, giving smart marketers a real reason to rediscover the medium.

If you want your message to be read over a cup of Joe in the peace and quiet of the potential purchaser's home, don't light up the keyboard and hit *Send*. Instead, look to the past for a new way to break through the clutter. Tell the youngsters in the office that you're kickin' it old school with the USPS.

If you want to reach your shoppers in the Internet age, sometimes you have to lick a few stamps.

Nike Ad? It Should Have Held That Tiger

Like millions of Americans, I was surprised (but not shocked) when Nike Golf aired a commercial featuring Tiger Woods during his catastrophic personal and professional implosion.

As a marketer, I want to shed some light on how Nike may have found its way to the exploitive "dad back from the grave" commercial. The motivation for the TV spot had little if absolutely nothing to do with the big life lessons Tiger was taught by his father. (It's been rumored for years that Earl also enjoyed the company of women other than his wives, so maybe there is some truth in the question from Earl, "Did you learn anything?"—but I digress.) No, father/son man-love and life coaching weren't the spot's drivers. Nike was simply attempting to stop the financial bleeding of the biggest endorsement deal known to golf. Bringing Earl back from the hereafter as a voice within Tiger's soul was just the most convenient and heartstrings-wrenching way its agency could dream up.

Reading the morning papers, I realized the power of Nike spin in full effect. Fresh out of a sex addiction clinic, Tiger is a changed man. Nike decided to play a nasty lie rather than taking a stroke penalty. Whether the corporation likes to admit it publicly or not, Tiger was, is, and will forever be the heart of Nike Golf, for better or worse. Like Gatorade (albeit a ton more successful than it in the pre-scandal days, and with a fortune more in the game), Nike built a brand specifically for Tiger in a category that had never experienced a sales-driving superhero of his magnitude. Tiger has made hundreds of millions for Nike, and the corporation would really like to have its breadwinner back at full strength sooner rather than later.

So the ad agency sat down with Nike and decided to bring Earl back from the grave to serve as Tiger's Obi-Wan Kenobi. The agency and Nike took the risk that no one had heard of the Earl rumors, or that if they had they wouldn't make the connection or care. By having the deep-voiced Earl seemingly challenge a critical cognitive step in Tiger's life journey, the son was once again the student, out to prove something to his father. The advertising sleight of hand was meant to redirect potential purchasers from the adultery to a higher, almost Zen-like challenge set by his father. By centering Tiger on the philosophical aspects of his life's purpose, shoppers wouldn't remember the more than a dozen party girls he liked to bed in hotel rooms around the world.

So why did Gatorade wait to cut ties with Tiger, and why did Nike decide to keep the partnership? Gatorade waited, most likely, to see how much Gatorade Tiger product it could get off the shelves before it pulled the deal. PepsiCo gave it several months, and then cut its losses. The Tiger product was a sales bomb anyway, so it wouldn't have lasted even without the scandal. Nike Golf didn't want to part ways with the man that single-handedly established the brand, so it decided to weather the storm. Go into any sporting goods store or golf shop and see what Tiger means to Nike. Nike's only real financial choice was to keep the man, regardless of well-publicized personal failings.

The success of Nike's Earl/Tiger commercial gamble will hinge on its reception by key consumer groups. If Suzie Shoppers pull the majority of Tiger Nike product, Nike will have to depend on the nag factor from their husbands or boyfriends to get the Suzies on board. If males make up most of Nike Golf's consumer base and the vast majority of them don't care about the adulteries enough to stop buying product, Nike's in the clear. Beyond the spot (which will have little if anything to do with the brand's fate long term), there's always consumers' water-under-the-bridge mentality. After enough time goes by, people might soften and Nike Golf and Tiger will be back on a winning streak.

What could Nike have done instead of running the father back from the dead spot? It could have sat the dance out. Taken a quiet high road. Waited until Tiger's winning ways won him back in the hearts/minds of Americans who tend to forget the sins of a winner. Instead, Nike dusted off an emotive bulldozer and plowed into its current and potential male consumers. (Its media buy for the spot, thus far, is male targeted.)

Nike also could have chosen a mea culpa spot. Mind you, people probably would have seen it as artificial hype, but it was an option. Sitting the dance out would have been more logical. Some might say that the added buzz created by the spot (every news network has mentioned it and it's all over the Internet) made the commercial worth it. Those people are probably the same ones who believe there's no such thing as bad publicity. Here's a newsflash: there is. That's how old Tiger got into this sponsorship mess in the first place. If Nike is viewed as insensitive by its target consumers, it will backfire.

Nike Corporation derived its name from the Greek goddess Nike, who is probably turning in her mythological grave over the irony of this mess. She is the deity of strength, speed, and victory, not of adulterous endorsers. Nike the corporation can only hope that Tiger's strength under pressure and a speedy win at the Masters will turn into sales victory at the register once again. Nike should have realized that it didn't need the Tiger/Earl commercial. Tiger's performance on the course, not in front of the camera, will be what changes Nike and Tiger's fortunes.

Bad News Couldn't Have Come at a Better Time for Toyota

If you're an automotive company dealing with a massive recall, pray for a bad economy and look to maximize your opportunities.

If bad was going to happen to Toyota, its timing couldn't be better. It's public knowledge that there aren't many people entering the new car market these days. Like other automotives, Toyota isn't missing out on much. If the economy was healthy, the PR nightmare of such an enormous recall could potentially be devastating. In a poor economy, however, people are much more apt to hold on to their cars for longer, looking to repair rather than buy. This buys Toyota much-needed time.

The average ownership in a good economy is several years, and even longer when things go south. Current Toyota owners affected by the recall purchased their cars in recent years, so it's fair to estimate they'll be holding on to them for several years to come even if the economy improves. This gives time for memories to soften, and gives Toyota a real opportunity—yes, I said opportunity—to grow a loyal following in the process.

True, dealerships have been faced with repairs in the tens of thousands. But many Toyota owners probably last saw their dealership when they purchased or when the warranty was running out, choosing instead to get servicing done for potentially less money elsewhere. And this, if the company can think on its feet, spells opportunity for Toyota.

Typically the most profitable area at a car dealership is its service department. Toyota has a chance to win owners back (and drum up some business in the process) with strategic interpersonal intervention. In order for Toyota to succeed, the owners who come in for recall repairs need to feel appreciated. Dealerships can do this in a number of ways, with the hopes of turning a negative experience into a positive one that can continue for the life of the car ownership.

When owners arrive, offer a free car wash. Their time is valuable, and most dealerships have car washes. Provide beverages and snacks while they wait. Have the head of sales or another dealership bigwig offer them Toyota's sincere apology. To get them back for service within six months, a move they probably wouldn't make on their own, give owners a free basic inspection certificate. (Coupons don't work as effectively as certificates or gift cards, especially with men.) The bounce-back effort will allow the service department the opportunity to have a positive interaction with the owner, and give the dealership an opportunity to sell additional products and services. It also probably wouldn't hurt dealerships to announce that, because of hard economic times, they've lowered their service department pricing for loyal Toyota owners. Every bit of good news will help improve shopper perception.

After an owner returns home with his/her repaired car, send a letter cosigned by the dealership owner and the head of the service department. Any actions that make owners feel that their initial purchase decision was not in error will help them reconcile their feelings about the brand. Next to a home, a car is the biggest purchase decision most shoppers make, and they don't want to feel that they made a huge mistake.

Toyota corporate let dealerships and owners down. If it acts quickly, however, it has a chance to make things right.

Client Death by E-mail

Interpersonal experts believe that basic communication is over 80 percent nonverbal. We watch facial cues and body language to see how our audience is reacting to our message. After nonverbal cues, we listen. Vocal inflections deliver emotional values as well as information. What we see and hear helps us to determine our actions and reactions within the conversation.

In marketing, just as it is in most of the business world, lightning-fast keystrokes and a quick press of *Send* can seem the model of client/agency efficiency. The more e-mails we write or answer, the better job we're doing. If the message is overlooked, misinterpreted, in need of further explanation, or lost, however, we're anything but efficient. And, if our feigned efficiency has taken away the opportunity for conversation and persuasion, the marketing product as well as the client/agency relationship may be in jeopardy. We must keep in mind we're in the business of sales, not speed, no matter how seemingly inconvenient a notion this might be.

When we rely on e-mails to do agency/client business, we risk misunderstanding what colleagues are really thinking. An e-mail can't replace a phone conversation. A phone conversation can't replace a video conference. A video conference cannot replace face-to-face. When we lose the visual and vocal cues, we risk missing the meaning entirely.

Certainly, the need for time efficiency in our business society is of critical importance. When it comes at the price of true efficiency (getting a good job done expeditiously with the minimum amount of back-and-forth commentary and unnecessary revisions), e-mail and voice mail and texting may not be appropriate solutions. If you're fast and fail, after all, you're not being efficient.

Agency/client interpersonal communication builds trust in ways that e-mails can't. E-mail doesn't lend itself to persuasion or debate or explanation, and doesn't fully afford the opportunity to share expertise. Often it takes longer through e-mail to get to a finished product, wasting valuable time and effort that could be better spent growing the client relationship and looking for new sales opportunities for the agency.

E-mail misinterpretation could be a book in itself. It seems everyone has a story about the e-mail that was given emotional value it didn't deserve or wasn't understood as intended. Even though it may seem interactive, an e-mail chain is a series of one-way conversations linked together via the Internet. Certainly, this is not the best way to form a discussion about important business issues. Further, unlike phone conversations or face-to-face meetings, e-mails may be forwarded. We lose control over the messages we e-mail the moment we send them, and may have no idea who else will be privy to the information.

It's often said that time constraints make it impossible to speak with clients on the phone or see them in person. Clients, overburdened by their workloads, might not even afford agencies time for a visit or call. Yet, by being too busy to meet away from the computer, the client may be doing the product/service a disservice by inadvertently racking up unnecessary agency hours. "If progress keeps progressing," a colleague lamented, "we may get to a point where we don't get any work done at all."

There is a big difference between sharing expertise and order taking. When agencies limit their exposure in front of clients, they risk losing their place as experts in the room. E-mails and voice mails are information sharers, not conversations. Client business is rarely won through e-mail, but it most certainly can be lost.

Some have perfected the art of the CYA (Cover Your Ass) e-mail. If we're using e-mail for self-protection, we need to look at a bigger client/agency or colleague issue. Fear of confrontation with or presenting to clients can also make e-mail seem like a viable option. Instead, it can adversely affect the client/agency relationship.

"If you want to grow business," I was told by an agency veteran years ago, "you'd better walk your client's halls." In today's challenging economy, it's even more critical that we put in the legwork.

Hit the Brakes on Price Breaks

Smart promotion marketers are always on the lookout for ways to apply key learnings between business channels. What you learn by moving cereal off the shelves might help you sell more seats on an aircraft, and salad dressing successes can move shoes. Conversely, marketers can also learn what missteps to avoid in a particular channel by the lessons learned from an unrelated shopper stream.

Consider, for example, lessons from the quick-service restaurant (QSR) sector on the short-term benefits and potential long-term risks associated with ninety-nine-cent pricing of "menu anchors" (core products). Ask anyone at McDonald's how much they'll get for menu anchor Big Mac in the near, medium, or supersized future, and they'll tell you: no more than ninety-nine cents. Such pricing is a proven short-term traffic and sales driver; as a bonus, customers buying the low-priced Big Mac might also want regular-priced fries and a drink. But there's long-term risk in marrying the notion of price directly to value.

Over time, such a strategy can overshadow other product attributes (quality, taste), and cannibalize more profitable menu items. If used too long or too often, price discounting is no longer a reward, but standard fare.

Right now, there's no shopper channel rolling bigger dice with pricing discounts than the automotive industry. With millions of dollars spent by a host of factories touting similar messages for months and even years, with no "limited time" end in sight, shoppers have stopped feeling a need to take immediate action. Result? Customers believe the real value of any car is price-minus-money-back, not the true price-equals-value equation. And, unlike QSRs that discount only select products to boost sales, many auto companies have no full-priced place to turn.

During a new SUV introduction, one auto exec I met expressed his disdain of customers who looked beyond the quality of his new, affordably priced SUV. They were most interested in cash-back incentives. His factory had spent millions of dollars over two years evangelizing the cash-back/0 percent APR message with every other model in the line, and yet he was honestly surprised and frustrated by customers' expectations. Rather than looking for ways to wean customers off price-break expectations, the majority of car companies seem to think the solution lies in a highly toxic combination of more advertising announcing even bigger cash-back incentives.

Customers can be weaned off cash-back incentives over time through added-value promotional initiatives. The key is delivering high-perceived value in keeping with brand image. This can be done via either an overt tie-on (such as free gas for a year with purchase of a fuel-efficient vehicle) or complement (minivan sales incentive awarding family DVD sets and a portable DVD player to buyers). It's all about perceived value. Selling to young adults? How about an upgraded sound system, an MP3 player with a thousand free music downloads, and $500 cash back (actual retail value of $2,500 that might cost the factory less than $1,000), rather than simply $1,500 cash back? Customers feel they've actually received more value at a price that saves the factory money, and at the same time the brand is building equity. Provided the perceived value is high in the minds of shoppers, it is a winning proposition that's financially smart.

Along with sales incentives, don't forget to drive traffic. If you're a car company that knows one out of ten test-drivers purchase, look to "brand true" promotional ideas designed to increase test-drives of potential shoppers. Test-drives combined with sales incentives in a clear, consistent promotional effort give dealerships the best opportunity to reach and sell key shoppers.

Recently, I was speaking with an advertising exec about a test-drive incentive for his automotive client. He stressed how important it was to protect the client's brand image and avoid decimating the brand that the agency had worked so hard to build. I asked about the effect the factory's cash-back bonus messaging had on the brand. He answered, "Well, we try not to think about that."

Now is probably as good a time as any to think about it.

The Ups and Downs of Product Placement

As TiVo and other digital recording services redefine TV viewership, many marketers are paying more attention to product integration through placement. Producers of reality shows such as *Extreme Makeover: Home Edition* and *Monster Garage*, and even talk shows like *Oprah*, use placement to build revenues for a show and secure bartered products for the program (such as appliances for a home makeover). Since placements seem less like advertising and more like a thread within creative, brands find that such integrations allow a softer sell to customers, plus an inferred celebrity or expert endorsement.

Nice, but brands weighing their placement options should be wary of the pitfalls, namely shopper backlash and vague ROI.

Viewers are savvy, and resent being oversold when experiencing their entertainment. If the placement is unnatural, too frequent, or in a group of too many other placements (see WB's *Space Jam*), marketers risk negatively impacting their brands. Fit is critical, so marketers must read scripts and ask the right questions. At the same time, entertainment content providers (producers, writers) should protect brands' interests. A brand that's burned in terms of response or placement cost won't return.

Then there's ROI. Ask the ultimate "end of the day" marketing question: did the placement help you motivate customers to take a specific action? Borrowed equity and celebrity endorsement can help build emotional attachments between brand and target audience. But how does that "feeling" weigh against the cost? Long past are the days when advertising and marketing budgets didn't insist on measurable results. Now, the key buzzwords are "financial efficiencies" and "quantifiable customer impact (QCI)."

To get a truly effective product placement, aggressively exploit tactics that not only endear customers, but motivate them to take immediate action. Product placement tied to smart promotional strategies closes the loop, and delivers quantifiable results that help determine ROI. Placements that don't include promotional extensions are incomplete.

Pontiac got great exposure last year when Oprah Winfrey gave away its cars to her audience. But the program would have been *much* stronger if it had closed the loop with a promotional overlay to Pontiac dealerships. What if everyone who took a test-drive received Oprah's latest Book Club selection? What if, for every test-drive taken during the promotional period, Pontiac made a donation to Oprah's Angel Network? What if everyone who took a test-drive registered to win a dream trip to Harpo Studios, lunch with Oprah, and her very own Pontiac? Brand awareness is nice, but getting shoppers to act (in this case, take test-drives) can be a natural and lucrative extension.

Take care when assigning the bookend roles of placement and promotion planner. It's not the primary responsibility of a media buying company to design your promotions. Even a product placement agency may not be right if it doesn't think promotionally. Promotional marketing agencies with proven track records executing entertainment partnerships are good places to start.

Most marketing pundits agree that product placement will play a much larger role in the years to come. By closing the loop via strategic promotional executions that deliver quantifiable results, marketers will reach and surpass product placement expectations and program goals.

Take It from Ray Kroc: There's Money to Be Made in the Air

Fast-food luminary Ray Kroc looked at every environment where shoppers and their wallets were present as a sales and service opportunity. *Give them what they want, when they want, the way they want it, and they will buy it.* From innovator Ray's point of view, there was no good reason not to sell and serve. If he were running America today, you can bet there would be sales in the air. And he'd call his sales and marketing strategy "airtail."

Airlines have yet to consider the true value of onboard sales and service. Rather than deliver on the wants/needs/desires of the shoppers, they undersell and under-market.

Here are just a few ways airlines can increase revenues in the air:

Develop a revenue-generating "buy on board" food/drink strategy.

Peruse just about any buy on board card and you'll find a Turkish market olio of snack choices: Brand X trail mix, a giant cookie, or a snack box containing a processed spreadable cheese product and a tubular meat product that, unwrapped, would surpass the life expectancy of diapers in a landfill. What are the top five prepackaged snacks that Suzie and Sam Shopper buy at retail? By supplying the products that shoppers actually want, the airlines can increase profitability and shopper satisfaction.

Some might suggest that airlines choose cart items based on profit margins. However, when the airline can't move product, the margin play becomes moot. People will buy more of what they like, and will feel better about the airline because of it. The airlines, tracking sales, will know what items to keep and discontinue. And, with proper planning, can figure out how to avoid shortages and plan accordingly. Running out shouldn't be a fear initially but a goal. Only then can the airlines realize true demand and supply it.

Offer items for purchase throughout the flight.

Airlines should provide opportunities to purchase as often as possible during a flight, not simply the one or two times when the cart is scheduled up and down the aisle. Virgin America's genius, its anytime menu and drink ordering offering, has turned its buy on board service into a win for both shoppers and the airlines. Passengers simply order from the screen on the seat back, swipe their cards, and their choices are delivered to them. It's efficient and cost-effective, while satisfying shoppers and delivering sales. (If the airlines are worried about the flight attendants' reactions, give them a guaranteed sales incentive for their efforts.)

Introduce a potent in-flight advertising vehicle.

The airlines have tried to crack the in-flight advertising nut for years, with varying degrees of success. Despite all their efforts, the biggest media-rich ad solve has yet to be successfully utilized. Perfectly positioned at eye view, a plane's overhead compartments are ideal spaces for print advertising. As passengers wait to take their seats or deplane, queue for the bathroom, or simply sit in their seats, they while away valuable minutes. Print ads housed in easily interchangeable frame systems would bring billable media value to airlines. City buses and subways have displayed similar print ads for decades, with a great deal of success.

The in-flight world, in the hands of retail-savvy marketers, is one of endless possibilities.

Imagine it: Southwest announces a brand-true "Vegas Starts Here" in-flight campaign. United sells "Sunshine at 35,000 Feet" for spring break. Virgin's offerings are so enticing, people don't want to deplane.

By giving travelers more of what they want and just enough of what they'll tolerate, the airlines can create an airtail environment that sells.

The Marketing of God: When Hellfire and Damnation Aren't Enough

Without argument, God marketing is the grandest and longest running of all sales initiatives. Unique in its variety of brand promises, religious marketing offers a maelstrom of perceived rewards and dangers combined with a plethora of folklore, fact, and faith. But crack the nut, and a motivated flock can take your brand well into the hereafter.

For even the best of Creatives, religion is a complicated sell. Marketers need only look to the '80s boom of the megachurches across America to know that it is possible to create a massive consumer following within the space. The search for meaning in a human's life is as old as life itself, and those claiming to know exactly how to find it can be quite enticing to consumers. However, establishing and keeping a flock (as witnessed by the recent downfall of the Crystal Cathedral and not-so-recent ebbing of the Catholic faith) takes strong retention (keeping them in the seats) and acquisition (bringing them there in the first place) strategies.

The number of Americans regularly engaged in organized religion has been free-falling in past decades. Taking the religious sales environment from a purely business point of view, it is a challenge not unlike ones faced by products and services the world over. A brand that does not hear and respond to its shoppers, regardless of the product's assets, risks extinction. Even a god or gods are not exempt from the power of shopper appreciation or competition for their devotion.

When marketing fails, brand managers must consider two major areas of contention: product attributes and shopper benefits. If the product itself doesn't deliver a value to the shopper, it can't be successfully sold. And a superior product will fail, regardless of its merit, if it isn't communicated in an appealing manner to the right audience at the right time within the shopper's purchase cycle.

Marketers are typically wary of product formula or product marketing changes, thinking that they will lose their base shopper in the process. This poses a unique challenge to time-tested religions that base their messaging on documents thought to have been divinely inspired thousands of years ago. Do you change with the times and risk losing your base, or risk extinction when fewer people want to hear your message?

Often the answer lies in targeted shopper research. Bringing the mountain to Mohammed by discovering his wants/needs/desires and marrying them to where it intersects church philosophy can help to develop a strong platform from which to jump. Maybe Joe Parishioner doesn't care a whole lot about life after death. Instead, maybe he just wants to get through the one he's living. Acme Church might consider pulling the emphasis from the hereafter and replacing it with the here and now. Making one's life better is what consumer products are all about, after all. Finding where Joe lives and what is important to him will light the path for those looking to fill the pews.

Arguably, there's not a more competitive marketing environment (or profitable service industry) in America than organized Christianity. Unlike unholy products that look to identify their USPs (Unique Selling Propositions), religion must find its DSP (Divine Selling Proposition). What makes one church, synagogue, mosque, or arena better than the one across the street? The consumers have more choice in religious experience than ever before, making the need for differentiation all the more important.

Unlike past generations, religious outlets simply telling consumers what to believe is not enough. Religions must listen to what consumers believe is important, find the product benefits within the religion that serve their needs, and communicate that successfully to the audience.

In the past, religions prospered simply by giving shoppers Hell. Today, it simply doesn't sell as well.

When to Be Social and How to Use It to Sell

Using social media to market products/services without a strong sense of basic marketing strategy is like operating a car without the steering wheel. Certainly, you can make the car move forward. However, the consequences could be anything from acceptable to disastrous.

Small business owners and managers interested in social media marketing have a twofold challenge: 1) they need to know how to easily and affordably use the new media, and 2) they need to be privy to basic marketing strategies that will work within the arena. Simply understanding the media isn't enough to guarantee sales success.

The top-selling books researched explain how one might enter into social media marketing, but emphasize the vehicle (social media) more than the driver (marketing). Small businesses must know how to implement specific marketing strategies in each social media format if they hope to increase awareness and sales. Knowing how to use the media is critical. Without seasoned expertise on marketing tactics that work, however, it is a wasted effort.

By focusing more heavily on how to use the medium rather than how to form successful marketing strategies within each social media format, we do ourselves a disservice and risk wasting time and money. If the marketing plan doesn't meet the needs/wants/desires of the consumer, it will fail, regardless of how flawlessly the actual tweet or update is executed.

When social media came on the scene, many wanted to (and did) jump instantly on the bandwagon, without much thought to marketing strategies and consumers' wants/needs/desires. Social media is a vehicle that smart marketers can use to engage consumers and promote a variety of brand-driving actions. If executed improperly, it can miss them entirely.

Without an intimate understanding of targeted consumers and their wants/needs/desires, the best marketing plans risk failure. Will they be convinced that the product should be engaged through social media marketing, or will it be a disconnect? With what frequency will they feel the message will be relevant to them? Does the reader want to reach the same consumers regularly, or continue to mine for new opportunities? Will the target audience even be willing to participate in social media, regardless of the carrot? Unlike traditional advertising, consumers choose to hear the message and want to engage the vehicle of social media.

It's imperative to have a solid marketing foundation before jumping into social media. It is an engaging vehicle, but if the company doesn't understand how its audience thinks, it won't be able to meet its marketing goals/objectives.

Men Are in Marketing, Women Are at Retail

The vast majority of marketing decisions for shopper products are made by corporate and ad agency men, and the vast majority of consumer product purchase decisions are made by women. Consider this: do we really think that men know women as well as women do?

In the '70s, marketing innovators such as McDonald's hired agencies owned and operated by Hispanics and African Americans to reach their respective ethnic populations. After all, the experts surmised, who could better understand those populations than members of said populations? Yet, when dealing with the nation's largest purchasing population, the female population, corporate America and agencies rely on men to make the vast majority of critical decisions to reach the female shopper. You need only look at the male-laden management rosters of agencies and shopper products corporations to see this truth.

Psychology experts believe that there is substantially less of a difference between the various male or female ethnic populations than there is between genders. Simple logic would assert that, when attempting to reach and influence a female population, those best equipped to make key marketing decisions are female. Whereas my male colleagues might not find this to be a great idea, given the exceedingly high number of female-driven products, it is a truly shopper-centric proposition.

If you want to sell more to the female population, it makes common sense to place women in agency and corporate management positions where they can make the final marketing decisions regarding products that are predominantly purchased by women. Women are less allured by the "sexiness" of a hot ad campaign or the latest pro athlete who wants to sign a soup deal. If the job is to sell to another female, women are best equipped to figure out how to do it. That's not to say that men can't, but that women are better suited for it.

Recently, a male member of a major retail corporation's sales force explained in a meeting that Oprah Winfrey and Ellen DeGeneres weren't good choices for use in the company's promotional marketing campaigns. Both celebrities test extremely well with women, and yet the sales force guy said he couldn't sell a program featuring either celebrity to his retailer group because they were too "controversial." The salesman's inability to step out of his own gender and bias to embrace the wants/needs/desires of the target audience adversely affected his ability to be successful.

A marketer at a major automotive company made a large sponsorship and media deal with a television sports program. The research had shown without doubt that the hefty majority of cars his company sold were to women, many of whom were single mothers. Although women watch baseball, it certainly wasn't the sweet spot of the target. Further, the executive didn't have a lot of money to burn on ineffective media buys. So why did he sponsor a baseball show? Because he liked baseball, and so did the guys from the ad agency who worked for him. When pressed about his rationale, he said simply, "Oh. We think it's a growth area." Growth areas are great if you're already delivering to your target, and a waste if you aren't.

Working on a children's marketing program in the '80s, experts guided the choice of toys that were given away as part of an added-value promotional effort. If you're going to make a toy and need to choose between a more boy-skewed or girl-skewed toy, they instructed, choose the Hot Wheels and leave the Barbie at home. Boys wouldn't play with girls' toys, but girls will cross the line and play with what would be considered a boy's toy. Girls don't fear the masculine in the way boys fear the feminine. The program was extremely successful, in large part because expert advice guided the decision making.

The research also showed that women are generally more empathetic, making it easier for them to understand the opposite gender than men. Female marketers, it can be argued, are better equipped to understand the point of view of male target audiences than men approaching female target audiences. Women are brought up to consider the wants/needs/desires of an entire family construct, whereas men are typically raised with a more male-centric, egocentric point of view. It may not be pretty to say such things out loud, but, according to psychologists, they're true.

At a large New York advertising agency, the women employees were asked to participate in focus group research. The topic? Feminine hygiene products. Several of their male colleagues who were leading a new business pitch for a feminine hygiene brand wanted us, the women, to share personal, intimate experiences in a conference while the men sat on the other side of a one-way mirror listening. Not surprisingly, no woman agreed and many were offended. Not understanding their audience, the men failed miserably in their quest for enlightenment.

Some skeptics may ask why any of this matters, or may try to write it off as feminist musings. It's actually a matter of sales. Let's say you own stock in Acme Corporation and it sells widgets. The shoppers who purchase 90 percent of Acme's widgets are female. Would you want the major marketing and sales decisions directly affecting this target made by a competent male or a competent female marketer? Now, before any men out there claim that they can fully understand women, think about how completely and totally you understand your wife or opposite gender significant other. One only needs to read the reams of research and best-selling books to see that women and men are wired differently (*Men Are from Mars, Women Are from Venus* or a host of others). Until more women are in decisive positions within marketing and sales forces, corporations risk not selling to their full potential because the shopper's point of view isn't fully understood or considered.

Understanding your shopper as deeply as possible and delivering against that understanding are the keys to successful marketing and sales strategies.

About the Author

Sarah O'Leary is known in the marketing industry as a passionate, seasoned creative expert.

During her twenty-plus-year tenure, she has executed strategic marketing initiatives for corporations including Wal-Mart, Hershey's, McDonald's, Kellogg's, Kraft, Toyota, and PepsiCo. Sarah has built a reputation for finding innovative solutions for a myriad of blue-chip corporate challenges.

Sarah enjoys addressing college classrooms and marketing conferences, spreading her own special brand of "marketing evangelism." She's also a regular contributor to *The Huffington Post* and her work is published occasionally in trade magazines.

The focus of her marketing beliefs and the premise of *Brandwashed* is this:

No matter how seemingly brilliant your marketing, it is worthless if it doesn't get shoppers to purchase your product.

Made in the USA
Lexington, KY
23 October 2011